D1130040

30 ST MARY AXE
A TOWER FOR LONDON

TLC
M.V. ELIZABETHAN
THAMES LUXURY CHARTERS LTD.
020 7378 1211
DIXIE QUEEN
LONDON

KENNETH POWELL
PHOTOGRAPHY BY GRANT SMITH

30 ST MARY AXE

A TOWER FOR LONDON

MERRELL
LONDON • NEW YORK

CONTENTS

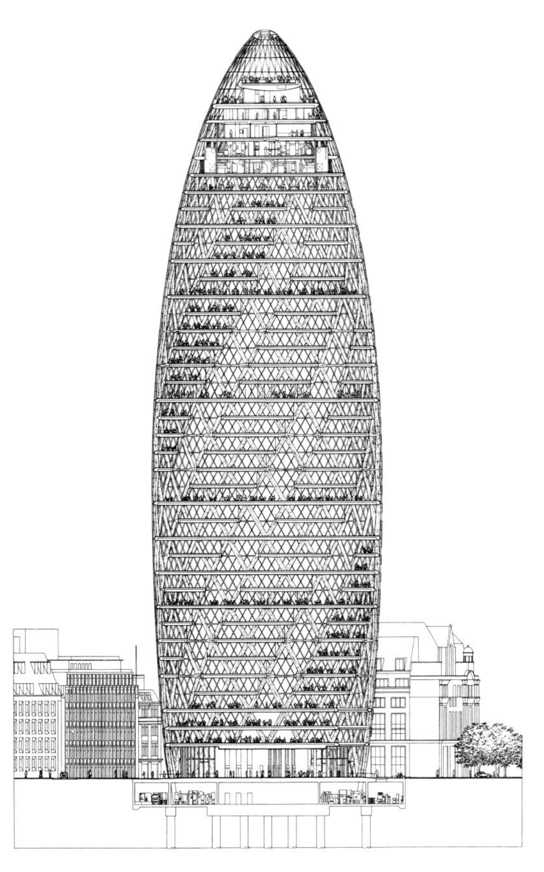

SITE AND DESIGN TEAM

SITE AND DESIGN TEAM

For Norman Foster, Lord Foster of Thames Bank, the Swiss Re tower in the City of London – 30 St Mary Axe, to give it its formal name – is "a tremendous act of faith and confidence in the future", a powerful statement about the future of the workplace and of the modern city. This is a building that reflects his progressive agenda for the design of office buildings, and is the latest in a line of iconic Foster office projects that includes the Willis Faber & Dumas headquarters in Ipswich, the Hongkong and Shanghai Bank in Hong Kong and the Commerzbank tower in Frankfurt. For Londoners it is simply the 'Gherkin'. Lord Foster, whose practice, Foster and Partners, won the coveted 2004 Stirling Prize (an annual prize for architecture, awarded to the architects of the building that has made the greatest contribution to British architecture in the past year) for the project, is happy with the nickname. "After all, it's a term of affection", he says. Equally happy is John Coomber, British-born former Chief Executive Officer (CEO) of the Swiss Reinsurance Company, known as Swiss Re, founded in 1863 in Zurich, where it still has its headquarters. "Get in a London taxi and ask to be taken to the 'Gherkin' and it's like asking for the Tower of London or Buckingham Palace", he says, "everybody knows it." For Coomber the building is not just a wonderful piece of publicity; it is equally one that reflects the core values of the company. "Swiss Re is about judgement and creativity", he says. "We're an ideas business and the London building epitomizes what we stand for."

Swiss Re began its move into the forty-storey tower at the end of 2003, less than three years after the start of construction. The history of the project, however, extends back into the 1990s, when the company became forcibly aware of the disadvantages of operating from five separate City buildings. As John Coomber says, the rationale behind the development of a bespoke new London headquarters was straightforward, a matter of "getting people to interact, exchange ideas, become a creative community". But procuring a new building on

Aerial view of 30 St Mary Axe.
Copyright © Guardian Newspapers Limited 2004.
Photographer Dan Chung.

Over thirty years Foster and Partners has pursued an innovative approach to workplace design, reflected in the Willis Faber & Dumas headquarters of 1975 in Ipswich (above left), the Hongkong and Shanghai Bank of 1986 in Hong Kong (left) and the Frankfurt Commerzbank tower of 1997 in Frankfurt (above).

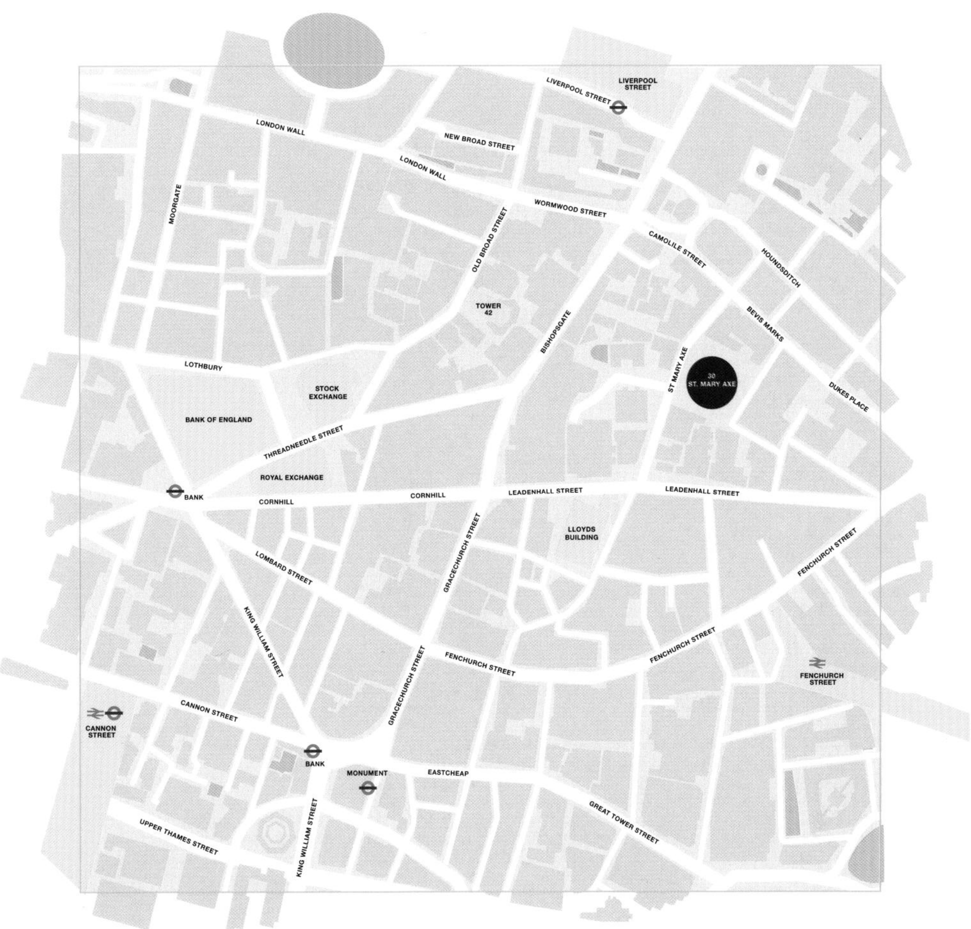

30 St Mary Axe is located in the heart of the insurance district, not far from Lloyd's of London.

the scale that Swiss Re required (up to 300,000 square feet) was not easy. London had been hit by a serious recession in the early 1990s. The property market took fright and many office projects were put on ice, so that when the recovery came there was a distinct shortage of high-quality office buildings to let in the capital. Swiss Re looked at a number of buildings, but none of those available came up to the required standard. There was never a real prospect of the company moving beyond the City – a relocation to Docklands, east London, was considered but ruled out – and there was a strong preference for a site close to the London insurance market in the eastern sector of the Square Mile, where insurance firms have long been rooted. In the end Swiss Re resolved to construct the building it needed in St Mary Axe, up the street from Lloyd's of London, designed by Richard Rogers and completed in 1986, and across the road from the Commercial Union (CU; now Aviva) tower of the 1960s, a City landmark of an earlier generation. For a company that is accustomed to dealing with the aftermath of disasters, there was a certain irony in the fact that the opportunity to obtain this site was effectively created by one of the worst terrorist outrages London had ever seen.

THE HISTORY OF THE SITE

St Mary Axe is a typically enigmatic name for a City of London street. It takes its name from the long-lost church of St Mary Axe, which allegedly possessed one of the axes used to slaughter St Ursula and her 10,000 virginal companions on their ill-fated visit to Germany. The church was closed and demolished in 1561. Even into the nineteenth century the street remained a respectable residential enclave until the tide of Victorian commercial development overwhelmed it. As late as 1883 the historic Golden Axe Tavern, mentioned in Charles Dickens's novel *The Old Curiosity Shop*, survived at the junction with Bevis Marks.

The Baltic Exchange arrived in St Mary Axe at the very end of the nineteenth century. The Exchange's origins lay in the mid-eighteenth century when merchants and ships' captains started to meet at a coffee-house in Threadneedle Street. Its business consisted of chartering and selling ships and putting shipowners in contact with those with cargoes needing transport. After the amalgamation of the Baltic Exchange with the London Shipping Exchange the newly enlarged organization bought the site of Jeffrey Square, off St Mary Axe, and commissioned the architects T.H. Smith and William Wimble to design a lavish new headquarters. Smith and Wimble were prolific commercial practitioners, active in the City between *c.* 1880 and the First World War. The budget

View of the Golden Axe Tavern at the corner of St Mary Axe.

Peter Paul Rubens, *The Martyrdom of St Ursula and the Ten Thousand Virgins*, oil sketch, 1602 (Palazzo Ducale, Mantua). St Mary Axe took its name from a church that housed an axe reputed to have been used to slaughter St Ursula and the virgins.

The Baltic Exchange, St Mary Axe façade, 1903.

for the new Exchange, completed in 1903, was generous, and high-quality materials were employed, with plenty of rich detail in carved stone, mahogany, marble and stained glass. The building was never, however, reckoned an outstanding work of its period. As *The Buildings of England* comments, "like much grand City architecture of that time, it was still entirely Victorian, untouched by Webb, Shaw, the Arts and Crafts, or any such influences". *Private Eye*'s 'Piloti', an indefatigable opponent of virtually any Foster project, described it (fairly) as "a decent, solid, turn of the century pile". ('Piloti' is a pseudonym of the distinguished architectural historian Gavin Stamp.) If the exterior of the building was pompously pedestrian, the Baltic Exchange's chief glory was the marble-lined central exchange hall, crowned with a glazed dome. This interior was certainly important as a survival of a City building type largely eradicated by post-war

The trading hall at the Baltic Exchange, one of a number of exchanges in the City of London where business was conducted face to face, 3 May 1920.

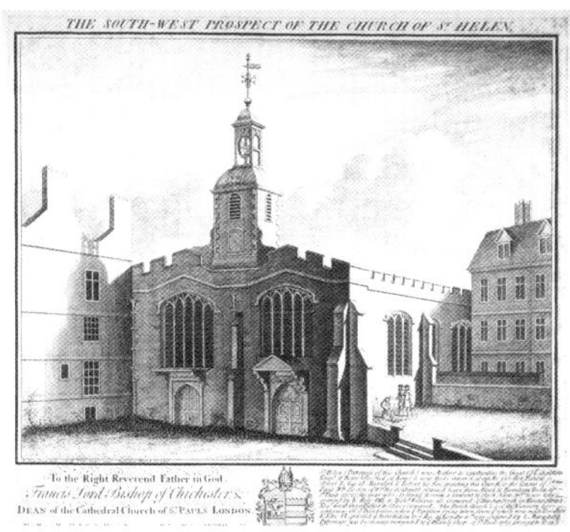

An engraving of St Helen Bishopsgate, showing the church from the west, 1736.

redevelopment: the Coal Exchange (1847–49) on Lower Thames Street was a famous casualty of the 1960s, a decade that also saw the demolition of the old Stock Exchange on Threadneedle Street. It was the splendour of the hall that rightly earned the Baltic Exchange a Grade II* listing. (It had been listed Grade II in 1972 and upgraded to Grade II* in 1987.)

By the 1990s the Baltic Exchange was one of the last vestiges of the Victorian redevelopment of the area, though the church of St Andrew Undershaft, on the junction of Leadenhall Street and St Mary Axe, and St Helen Bishopsgate, on Great St Helen's, were that far rarer commodity – medieval survivors of the Great Fire of 1666. Much of the west side of the street of St Mary Axe had been demolished for the 1960s joint CU/P&O development, with its Manhattan-style open plaza. Many other nineteenth-century buildings had been swept away in

St Andrew Undershaft and the view along St Mary Axe, 1911.

Both the Commercial Union building of 1969 (far left) and Lloyd's of London of 1986 (left) were considered radical in their time.

the boom years of the 1980s, replaced by new developments in the then-fashionable Postmodernist manner, none of them of any special distinction. These buildings were as typical of their era as the Victorian commercial palazzi they replaced: Postmodernism became, for a time, the City style, a reaction, perhaps, against the radicalism of Richard Rogers's Lloyd's at the end of St Mary Axe.

On the evening of 10 April 1992 a bomb left by IRA (Irish Republican Army) terrorists, containing 100 lb of Semtex explosive, exploded close to the Baltic Exchange, the first of two IRA terror attacks on the City. (The second, almost equally disastrous, bombing took place in April 1993, when buildings in nearby Bishopsgate were devastated.) Three people, one of them a fifteen-year-old girl, were killed. The cost of repairing damage to property was estimated at up to £1 billion. The CU tower was among the buildings badly hit, but the Baltic Exchange took the brunt of the blast, with its St Mary Axe façade blown off and the interior extensively damaged. Following the approval of the Swiss Re project, Simon Jenkins, one of London's leading journalists and a passionate conservationist, suggested that the subsequent failure of the City to insist on the restoration of the Exchange was, in effect, a surrender to the IRA. After all, he commented, the medieval church of St Ethelburga, Bishopsgate, all but totally destroyed by the bomb in 1993, had been faithfully rebuilt. Why not the Baltic?

St Ethelburga's was, of course, a tiny building, the smallest of the City churches, and a very rare survivor of the Great Fire. The case for rebuilding it was overwhelming. But if the Baltic Exchange were to be rebuilt, who would fund it

Damage caused by the IRA bomb of April 1992 to the Commercial Union tower (below), as it was then known, and the Baltic Exchange (opposite) was extensive.

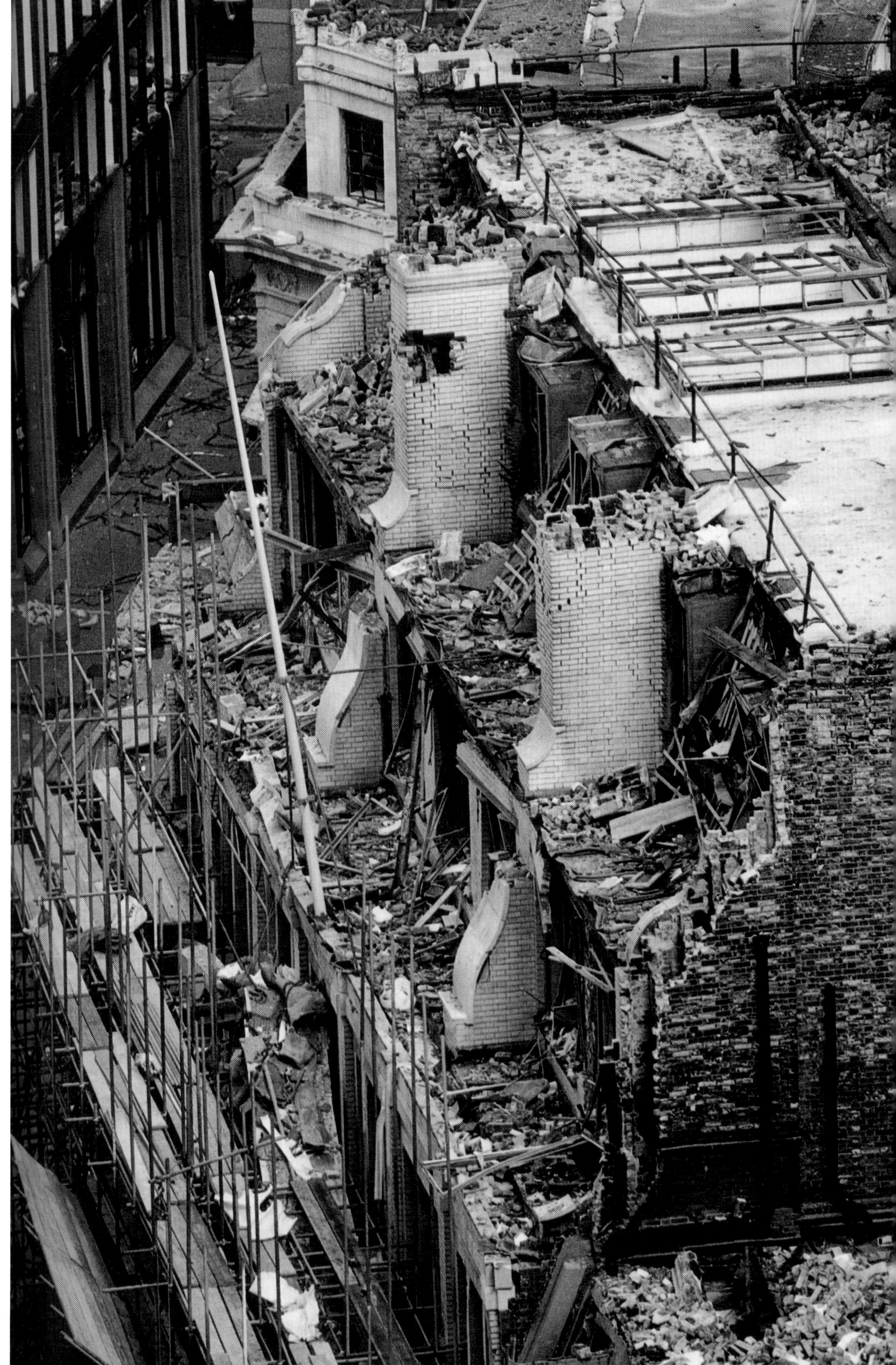

and for what end? Like other traditional City institutions, the Baltic Exchange was in transition if not decline, with much of its business increasingly done by electronic communication rather than face-to-face trading. Long before the bomb in 1992, the Exchange had first considered the option of moving its operations to a new site and later explored the possibility of a reconstruction that would incorporate the key historic elements of the building but also provide lettable office space and financial dealing floors. Both the City of London Corporation, as planning authority, and English Heritage, the government's adviser on the historic environment, were, however, keen to see the building restored and reluctant to see the badly damaged fabric destroyed. The exchange hall was regarded as particularly precious and should be retained in any future development of the site, it was ruled. It was also desirable that the St Mary Axe frontage be rebuilt. Paul Drury, then head of English Heritage's London Division, insisted in 1993 that the organization's main concern was "to ensure the reinstatement and restoration of the principal elements of the listed building".

St Ethelburga's is now a Centre for Peace and Reconciliation after its reconstruction.

For four years the site was in limbo as the City and English Heritage stuck to their ruling and the committee of the Baltic Exchange despaired of finding a commercially viable way of achieving restoration of the building. Meanwhile, action was taken to safeguard those parts that had survived the bombing. The remains of the damaged St Mary Axe frontage were carefully dismantled, packed up and stored off-site as the development options were explored. The damaged interior remained sealed up on-site until December 1994, when the Baltic Exchange sold the site, with the exchange hall still standing at its centre, to the developer Trafalgar House. Press reports suggested that the sale price had been £12.5 million. The Exchange's chairman, in a circular letter of October 1993, sent to all members, pointed out that the institution was operating at an annual loss of £1 million and that the damaged building could not be regarded as an asset. "A restoration and reoccupation by the Exchange of the listed building would not be in shareholders' interests ... We have

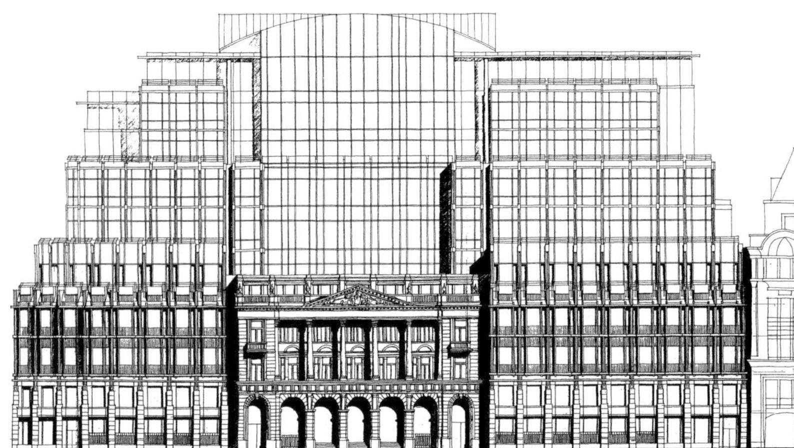

The GMW groundscraper scheme incorporated the original Baltic Exchange façade, but it was never built.

Self-contained winter gardens are a key feature of the Commerzbank in Frankfurt, 1997.

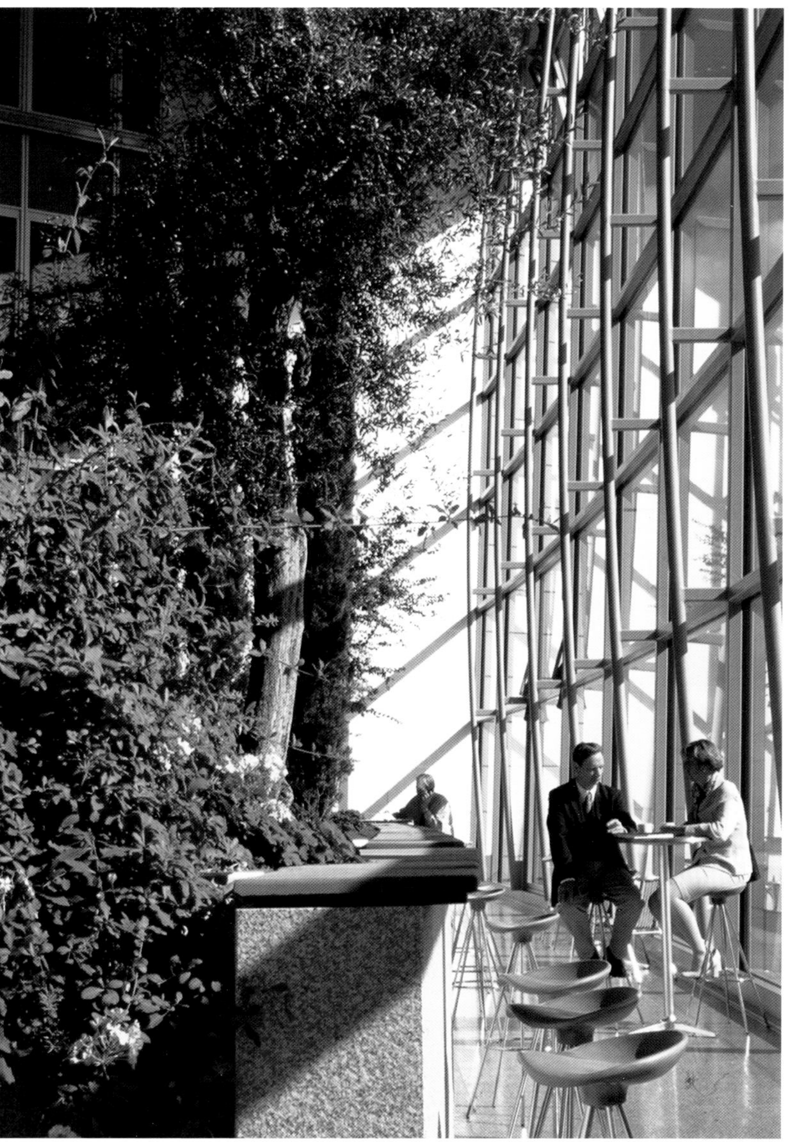

had proposed 'sky gardens' at the Hongkong Bank, but they had failed to materialize. In Frankfurt the gardens, with generous planting, channel natural light and fresh air via opening windows into the office floors. During much of the year the building can be naturally ventilated, with the cooling system of chilled ceilings (rather than conventional air conditioning) turned on only when the temperature inside rises beyond controllable limits or high winds rule out open windows. The form of the building, with the gardens stepped from one side to another as they rise up the tower, maximizes views into these green spaces and out to the city. Foster believes that one of the huge advantages that high buildings offer is the access to views. "Think of the way in which people's view of Paris changed when they could ascend the Eiffel Tower and see it from the top", he says.

A computer-generated image of the Millennium Tower on the City skyline, seen from the dome of St Paul's Cathedral (above left), and a photograph of a model of the tower from 1996 (above).

"The feedback we got from Commerzbank was that the energy-saving agenda, important as it is, is less important than the way the building is enjoyed by those who work there." If the Hongkong Bank was a reinvention of the tall office building, Foster can credibly claim to have repeated that feat in Frankfurt.

THE MILLENNIUM TOWER

With the GMW groundscraper project seen as a non-starter, Trafalgar House, succeeded by Kvaerner following a take-over in the spring of 1996, began to look at other options for the Baltic Exchange site. The immediate outcome was Norman Foster's London Millennium Tower project. Foster had been working since 1989 on another Millennium Tower intended to be constructed in Tokyo Bay. Some 840 metres tall and over 10 million square feet (1 million square metres) in area, the tower would house offices, hotels, apartments and leisure facilities; it would be, in effect, a self-contained vertical town of 50,000 people. The London Millennium Tower was projected as a more modest 385-metre-tall, 1,700,000-square-foot (160,000-square-metre) structure. Again it would be a mixed-use project, with offices, apartments and retailing, as well as a public observation deck 305 metres above the ground. The tower sharply divided opinion, generating expressions of outrage from the 'heritage' lobby, concerned at its skyline impact: the proposed tower would have been more than twice as high as the tallest building so far constructed in London, the NatWest Tower, later renamed Tower 42 (183 metres). For others, it was potentially a bold statement of London's identity as a global business capital. One major factor in its favour was that it would be located in a small area of the City where tall buildings could be, and had been, erected without intruding on protected view 'corridors', notably those safeguarded by the St Paul's Heights policy that the City itself had promulgated between the wars to protect the setting of St Paul's Cathedral. As Peter Rees confirms, however, the chances of the tower receiving planning consent were slim: it was simply too big.

But the Millennium Tower was notable for more than sheer scale. Rees compares the bifurcated top of the design to "a surprised rabbit", with two 'ears' forming a distinctive culmination to the tower. The building would have been served by a series of double-deck, high-speed lifts depositing passengers in 'sky lobbies'. Much thought was given to the environmental aspects of the design. There would have been 'sky parks' providing shaded green oases, and extensive use of natural ventilation and insulation to reduce the reliance on mechanical cooling. The possibility of drawing water from a spring deep in the ground beneath the building to assist in the cooling process was explored. The odds might have been stacked against the project, but it was developed with all the thoroughness for which Norman Foster is legendary. Foster still enthuses about the scheme, which, he says, was a bold attempt to create public spaces in the sky – bars, restaurants and galleries around green gardens – as well as outstanding office space and the best apartments in Europe. But he realizes that it was probably simply too radical for London.

In the summer of 1997 Foster produced a reduced version of the design for the Millennium Tower, no more than 300 metres tall. He believes that the project was winning increasing support and that the second scheme was achievable. Kvaerner, however, lost confidence in the project. The second version of the tower was never formally submitted for planning, and early in 1998 the entire project was

Much of the east of the City is outside designated conservation areas and is therefore the obvious location for tall buildings.

The site

Conservation areas

Listed buildings

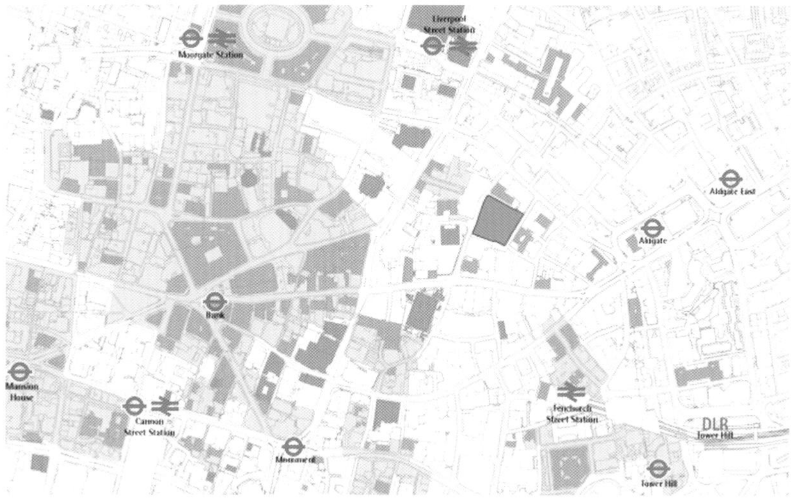

abandoned after Swiss Re had agreed to buy the site from Kvaerner, subject to planning permission being secured. "The client had already killed it: it could have been built", Foster comments, with some bitterness. Foster and Partners' involvement with the site, however, continued. Previous proposals for the site, including the GMW groundscraper scheme, had been viewed with dismay by Peter Wynne Rees and his colleagues. "There was a tradition in the City of going to the architect you knew – the same old practices got all the jobs and the result was often a lacklustre building. I wanted to see major talents like Foster working in the City."

Any redevelopment of the St Mary Axe site faced the major hurdle posed by the still-listed remains of the Baltic Exchange, partly stored off-site but with the exchange hall still boarded up at the centre of the site (see pp. 42–43). There had, however, been signs of a change of stance on the part of English Heritage and the City Corporation, allowing for the removal of the remains of the building if there was a prospect of an outstanding replacement. This strengthened the case for retaining Foster's services. The sale of the site to Swiss Re was entirely dependent on planning permission for a new building being given. Richard Griffiths had been Senior Vice President, Construction, with overall responsibility for the first phase of the huge Canary Wharf development in Docklands and was brought in by Swiss Re as a consultant to manage the St Mary Axe project; he recalls that the site was "messy: there was the problem of the remains of the Baltic and what should happen to them. And the issue of whether a high building would be allowed. But the problem rested with Kvaerner – they had to get planning permission before Swiss Re would seal the deal to buy the land." Swiss Re wanted a minimum of 400,000 square feet (37,200 square metres) of offices on the site, some of which was to be lettable.

The Foster team went back to the starting-point in considering the options for the site. Late in 1997 it had produced a sketch scheme for a building of almost 538,000 square feet (50,000 square metres), which featured floors considerably

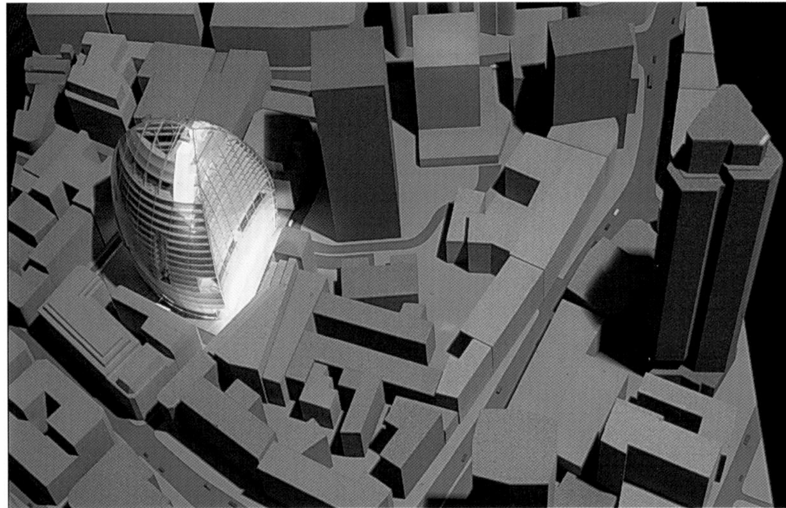

An early version of Foster and Partners' new design for the site, from 1997, was likened to a loaf of bread.

The GLA (Greater London Authority) building, known as City Hall, was erected south of the River Thames in 2002. The building features an internal ramp spiralling to the top floor (right).

larger than those on offer in the Millennium Tower project. No more than 110 metres high, its shape was described variously as "the loaf of bread" or "a glorified beehive". The design reflected a move in Foster's architecture away from the strictly orthogonal towards more flowing, organic forms: the City Hall project, won by Foster in competition in 1998, was a further reflection of this tendency, which emerged in several other office projects for the City of London. Working with Foster from the beginning of the project was the eminent engineering practice of Arup, the practice's collaborators on so many projects worldwide. As the scheme progressed, a series of expert consultants joined the team.

THE CLIENT

The reason for the foundation of the Swiss Reinsurance Company – Swiss Re for short – was an event little remembered today outside Switzerland. On 10–11 May 1861 the small town of Glarus was virtually destroyed by fire: 500 houses went up in flames and 3000 inhabitants were left homeless. Insurers were hit hard and three of them, the Helvetia General, Schweizerische Kreditanstalt (Credit Suisse) and the Basler Handelsbank, came together to establish Swiss Re, which was formally incorporated on 19 December 1863. The company's first office was a two-room apartment on Zurich's Schoffelgasse, a modest beginning for what became a global organization. But the idea of reinsurance (insurance for other insurance companies that spreads the risk of the direct insurer) proved a winner; within a couple of years it was being applied to the life insurance business as well as to the insurance of property and shipping. In 1913, to celebrate its fiftieth birthday, the company moved to new purpose-built offices at Mythenquai on the outskirts of Zurich, overlooking the lake. Much extended, the building, known as the Altbau,

The original façade of the Swiss Re Zurich headquarters of 1913 was retained in a recent remodelling that enclosed the central courtyard under a glass roof.

remains the headquarters of Swiss Re today. The company employs more than 3500 people in Zurich alone, but this city is just one of its operational bases. Worldwide, Swiss Re employs over 8000 people in 70 offices in more than 30 countries. A branch opened in Beijing in 2003. In 2004 Swiss Re became the first global reinsurer to commence full-scale operations in China.

The company is a major investor in world financial markets and its activities in London date back a long time. In 1916 it acquired a majority shareholding in a leading British reinsurer, Mercantile & General (M&G). M&G parted from Swiss Re in 1968 but in 1996 was acquired in its entirety for £1.7 billion, the two companies merging their operations. M&G was particularly prominent in the field of life insurance and had a large workforce based in the City of London, where Swiss Re had opened its first contact office in 1964. The 1996 purchase was a catalyst for Swiss Re's plans to rehouse its operations in a new building in London, and the acquisition in 1999 of London investment bank Fox-Pitt, Kelton meant that there was another group of staff to be accommodated.

London's particular importance to Swiss Re was that the city was home to the company's life and health division, an area of the reinsurance business in which Swiss Re was the acknowledged world leader – in four years the company's income from life insurance had nearly doubled. When the St Mary Axe project was being designed and built, John Coomber, who became CEO of Swiss Re in 2003, was running this operation from London. He was to become a firm supporter of the project.

Swiss Re is a company with a strong sense of mission. John Coomber speaks eloquently of its commitment to the principle of sustainability, which, he says, is "an absolute fundamental element of our business philosophy. It's also an important contributor to our long-term business success." Sustainability is one of Swiss Re's four core values. The reasons for its inclusion are clear. Climate change is triggering floods and droughts, changing the pattern of diseases worldwide and adding greatly to the uncertainty of human life. Swiss Re has an obvious interest in its consequences and has been sponsoring initiatives aimed at combating global warming, for instance reafforestation programmes. Its annual report contains, unusually, an analysis of the carbon dioxide emissions created per staff member. It is hardly surprising that Swiss Re responded positively to the idea of an environmentally friendly London building.

Nor is a concern for good design and the quality of the workplace a novelty in Swiss Re circles. The progressive extension of the Mythenquai headquarters has been carried out to a high standard, in terms of architecture, landscape and especially the integration of artworks. When the central courtyard of the building of 1913 was enclosed to form a glazed atrium commissions were given to three major artists: Carl Andre, for a striking floor sculpture, and Olafur Eliasson and Tatsuo Miyajima, for installations for the two lift shafts. Staff restaurants look out

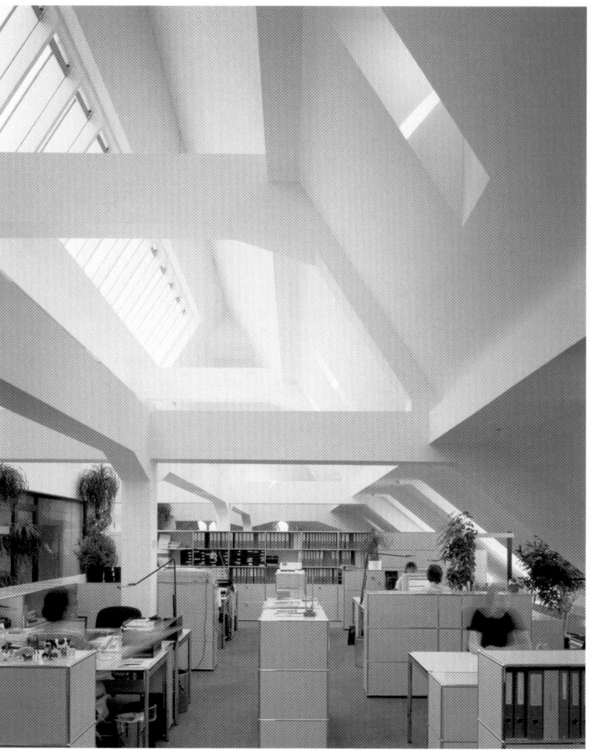

The renovation of the Swiss Re Zurich headquarters of 1913 opened up spaces in the top floor.

New lift shafts at the Zurich headquarters incorporate light installations by Olafur Eliasson and Tatsuo Miyajima, and a striking floor sculpture by Carl Andre in the central courtyard.

to the lake and offer cuisine that is several notches above the food provided in the typical office canteen. A few miles from Mythenquai, high above the lake, Swiss Re's conference venue at Rüschlikon – the Swiss Re Centre for Global Dialogue – is an outstanding marriage of new architecture and careful restoration. The core of the centre, used for meetings and conferences by many outside organizations as well as by Swiss Re, is a villa built in the 1920s by architects von Sinner and Beyeler, a charming creation in the spirit of the Bernese country houses of the eighteenth century, which has been carefully restored with a potent contribution to its interior by artist Günther Förg. The new additions by Zurich-based architects Marcel Meili and Markus Peter are outstanding for both their response to the site and the high quality of details, finishes and furniture, much of the last specially designed by the Vienna practice of Krischanitz & Czech. Rüschlikon is an inspirational place that expresses the ideals of Swiss Re, above all its commitment to quality and patronage of the best architecture, design and art.

Swiss Re's conference building at Rüschlikon merges the old with the new.

Carla Picardi, Project Director during the design and planning phase of the project, and Richard Griffiths, Project Manager.

Keith Clarke, former Chief Executive of Skanska.

THE SWISS RE TEAM

Having resolved to develop the St Mary Axe site with a new building housing all its London-based staff, and providing some lettable space in addition, Swiss Re set about assembling a team to work with its chosen architects. The core of the team had a strong North American bias, and there was a marked link to Canary Wharf, the booming Docklands office district that Swiss Re had briefly considered as a location. Carla Picardi, who had graduated from the University of Massachusetts with a degree in design and architecture and worked in the fields of development and facility management, had joined the Canary Wharf project in 1985 as Associate Director of Design and Construction initially for G. Ware Travelstead and subsequently for the developer Olympia & York, where she worked for Richard Griffiths. She remained at Canary Wharf until 1992, seeing the development explode in scale to challenge the City of London as the financial powerhouse of Britain. Picardi was awarded a Loeb Fellowship at Harvard and had no special desire to return to London, but the draw of the St Mary Axe development proved an irresistible challenge and she went back to London in January 1998. The Canary Wharf connection seemed to extend far and wide: Keith Clarke, Chief Executive of Kvaerner UK (and then, for a time, of its successor company, Skanska UK) and the man who sealed the site acquisition deal with Swiss Re, had also worked for Olympia & York. He was a trained architect and Picardi found him "a breath of fresh air", resolving potential issues between Kvaerner and Swiss Re.

"The appointment of Foster wasn't inevitable, despite his previous involvement with the site", says Picardi. "There was a commitment to an outstanding building,

but we could have gone to, say, Frank Gehry. We wanted exceptional architecture but had to find an architect we were comfortable with. In the end, we stuck with Foster." A steering committee was formed at Swiss Re to oversee the rapidly evolving project. It included John Coomber, then head of Swiss Re's operations in the United Kingdom, and the heads of the three London-based business groups: Ann Godbehere, from M&G in Canada, who was to become Group Chief Financial Officer in 2001; Rudi Glesti, a Zurich-based executive who had taken a close and informed interest in the company's building programme; and Sheree Whatley, the chief financial officer of one of Swiss Re's UK-based business groups and the woman who had hired Carla Picardi. "The project was a big gamble for Swiss Re", says Picardi. "Comparable organizations, Citibank, for instance, had looked at the site and turned it down. Some people were very nervous about the idea of doing a big City development." Sheree Whatley, Picardi recalls, was very

Above left
John Coomber, former CEO, Swiss Re, who led the project from its inception.

Top
Ann Godbehere, CFO, Swiss Re.

Centre
Rudi Glesti, Swiss Re.

Bottom
Walter Kielholz, Executive Vice Chairman, Swiss Re.

influential when it came to convincing the Swiss Re board that this was a good move. "She was a money person, able to analyse the costs and benefits, someone with a feeling for the instincts of the board and someone they trusted. She convinced them."

John Coomber remembers presenting the project to the Swiss Re board in Zurich. His conviction was that the new building, even before its form had been resolved, was vital to the business. "But the company was engaged with building projects in Zurich, Munich and the USA and it could have demurred from another large investment." Fortunately, Walter Kielholz, who was then Group CEO (later Executive Vice-Chairman), backed the idea strongly. Kielholz has a strong visual sense that goes beyond the typically Swiss taste for the clean and minimal. A table in his office is stacked with books on architecture and art. Its practical success apart, Kielholz dislikes Canary Wharf for its predominantly Postmodernist aesthetic. "One of the aspects of 30 St Mary Axe that pleases me is the way in which it has changed public attitudes and made London more receptive to innovative new design", he comments. The fact that the Prince of Wales disliked the building "only made us realize how good it was", he says.

With Swiss Re embarking on the battle to win planning permission, there were some tough discussions with the Foster team, in which Ken Shuttleworth (a former director who quit Foster and Partners in 2003 to establish his own practice) was involved alongside Norman Foster and, for a time, Andy Miller, another experienced senior member of the practice. The failure of the Millennium Tower project suggested that a much lower building would be required to win over the City. However, it would have to provide the requisite amount of floor space, though Swiss Re remained unclear exactly how much of the building it would occupy. Foster director Robin Partington assumed overall control of the project, leading what was recognized as an exceptionally talented design team.

Norman Foster (below), founder and chairman of Foster and Partners, and Robin Partington (below right), formerly of Foster and Partners.

The design process involved weekly meetings with the client, frequently lasting the entire day. Preparation for the meetings included plans, sketches, models, and even full-scale mock-ups of such key elements as the diagonal column casing.

Sara Fox, Project Director during the construction phase, and Peter Holroyd, Construction Director, Swiss Re.

Carla Picardi recalls that alongside the formal, extended planning negotiations with the City of London Corporation and English Heritage, not to mention many other bodies, including the Royal Fine Art Commission (RFAC) and the Commission for Architecture and the Built Environment (CABE), established in 1999, her job included a more subtle process of opinion forming. "We did a lot of schmoozing", she says candidly. There were meetings with politicians, but Picardi rejects a journalistic account in which the Prime Minister, Tony Blair, was lobbied personally to speed up the planning process. "As far as I'm aware, it just did not happen", she says. During the tense days of the year 2000, when a ratification by the Deputy Prime Minister, John Prescott, of the final planning permission given by the City Corporation was awaited, there was a meeting on 17 July with London Mayor Ken Livingstone and his deputy, Nicky Gavron. Livingstone, who had been elected on only 4 May of that year, did not have the power to derail the project by blocking planning consent or triggering an appeal process, but he could have influenced the outcome. But the Swiss Re team, which included Norman Foster and Malcolm Kerr (of DP9, then at Montagu Evans), found that he was highly positive, indeed enthusiastic, about the scheme. The City of London had expressed doubts about the creation of the office of Mayor of London and the extent of the incumbent's planning powers, but it was soon to forge an alliance with Livingstone to push through major new office schemes seen as vital to its future survival.

As preparations intensified for the start of construction, planned for late 2000 or very early in 2001, the Swiss Re team was substantially reinforced. Peter Holroyd, who had worked with Richard Griffiths in Canada, having moved there from Britain, married and started a family, was persuaded to return to London at the very end of 1999 as in-house Construction Director working directly with the contractor, Skanska, and with Foster and Partners. Sara Fox arrived in London in September 2000 to take up the post of Project Director with Swiss Re, her brief being to take over from Carla Picardi – the two women overlapped in office for around three months – and get the building built and occupied. Fox had worked for Olympia & York at Canary Wharf between 1989 and 1992, rising rapidly to become Vice-President for Administration. She had subsequently worked for Equitas at Lloyd's of London as a project manager, before moving to New York in 1995 to work for Swiss Re as Senior Vice-President (relocation). Her task there was to oversee the construction of Swiss Re America's new 300,000-square-foot (27,900-square-metre) headquarters in Armonk, New York (approximately 25 miles north of Manhattan). Working from New York, she was then drafted in as a member of the project steering committee for the new London headquarters.

If Carla Picardi had gained a reputation at Canary Wharf for persistence and persuasive powers that earned her the nickname of the 'velvet glove', Sara Fox was to be remembered by many team members as the 'iron fist' on account of her sheer determination and drive. Fox recalls her first weeks on the project as "a roller-coaster ride", attending the regular planning meetings with Carla Picardi, planning consultant Barnaby Collins (of DP9, then at Montagu Evans), Ray Jackson (of the legal firm Linklaters), the publicist Georgie Gibbs and others, and becoming imbued with the background and history of the project. "As soon as I was up to speed, I began asking awkward questions", she recalls. "I think my style was regarded as rather abrasive, let's say. I tended to say things like: why do we talk and talk – when are we going to be doing something?" Soon after her arrival in London, Sara Fox was faced by the unexpected obstacle of the legal action instigated by the campaigning group SAVE Britain's Heritage to prevent the building going ahead, although this was fortunately later aborted. The project finally went live on 3 January 2001, when the sale of the site to Swiss Re was formally completed and construction began. Swiss Re was contractually bound to use Skanska as the main contractor for the project, but the latter did not enjoy an easy ride. "We squeezed them", Fox recalls: Skanska finally agreed to build the tower in thirty-three months rather than the thirty-seven it had originally proposed.

Sara Fox's aim was to develop a project team with a strong culture of its own. One of Swiss Re's buildings on Leadenhall Street, in the City, became the base for a multidisciplinary team that included architects, engineers, project managers and contractors. "It was like a parallel universe where the guys on the job could separate themselves from the fetters of their own offices. Of course, there were disagreements sometimes, but gradually everyone started to work together and the project itself became everyone's focus." The project office was "a snakepit", Fox says, "but there was a real buzz to it". A good deal of that "buzz" was generated by Fox herself, whom everyone involved with the project credits with generating a rare sense of mission in the project team.

THE PLANNING PROCESS AND THE PUBLIC

The terrorist bomb in 1992 had left the Baltic Exchange and the City Corporation with a massive problem. The City Corporation wanted a redevelopment that would combine retention of the key historic features with some financial return in terms of lettable office space, but the scheme consented in 1995 did not seem likely to find a developer. The Baltic, despondent about the apparent impossibility of finding a viable development along these lines, had already decided to cut its losses and sell the site to Trafalgar House, later Kvaerner. The saga of the Millennium Tower followed, ending unhappily.

The Corporation was bound, as a planning authority, to seek the restoration of the damaged building, which remained listed, in line with the government's Planning Policy Guidance note 15 (PPG15). This insisted that "demolition of any Grade II* building should be wholly exceptional and require the strongest justification". The City could not, in any case, give consent for the demolition of any listed building; the matter would have to be referred to the government and the decision taken by the Secretary of State for the Environment. In the period immediately before the general election of 1997 in the UK, this office was held by the Conservative minister John Gummer. After the election to government of Tony Blair's New Labour, it passed to John Prescott, who combined it with the title of Deputy Prime Minister, heading a super-ministry called the Office of the Deputy Prime Minister from 2001. English Heritage would also have a decisive role in recommending whether consent for demolition ('listed building consent') should be given. In London it had the power to direct a local authority to refuse listed building consent, a direction that could be overruled only by the Secretary of State. A public inquiry, a procedure that could involve a legal hearing lasting weeks and a long delay in the announcement of a decision, was also possible.

During the 1980s two public inquiries had been held into the future of the site at the Bank junction in the City of London owned by Peter (later Lord) Palumbo. The proposal to site a tall office building there – a design by the renowned German architect Ludwig Mies van der Rohe (who had died in 1969) – together with a new public square was rejected after a hearing in 1984. A second inquiry, with the City Corporation, English Heritage and many others opposing a low-rise scheme by James Stirling (Number 1 Poultry) that would replace the existing group of listed buildings, resulted in victory for Palumbo. Sophie Andreae, who, as Chairman of SAVE Britain's Heritage, was heavily involved in the battle to save those buildings, was subsequently appointed head of English Heritage's London Division, a post she held at the time of the bomb of 1992 in St Mary Axe. She dispatched an Inspector of Historic Buildings and an engineer to the site of the blast, their mission being to determine what was left and whether the Baltic Exchange could be restored. "The Exchange was badly damaged, we discovered, but there was no doubt that it could be reinstated – most of the key decorative elements

The shell of the Baltic Exchange's central hall remained in situ until it was finally removed in early 2001.

The original Mappin & Webb building at Number 1 Poultry was replaced by a building designed by James Stirling.

were there. Our advice was that rebuilding was possible, and that anyone wishing to do otherwise would have to make a very good case." Andreae left English Heritage in 1993 – she subsequently served as a commissioner of both the RFAC and CABE – but she believes that the cases of Number 1 Poultry and the Baltic Exchange were very different. "The buildings Palumbo wanted to demolish were intact, occupied and could readily have been refurbished. The Baltic was wrecked. Rebuilding would be costly and the question was: who would pay and for what purpose?" Andreae considers that it was quite reasonable that four years after the bomb, with the site still lying fallow, English Heritage and the City Corporation should review their positions on the future of the building.

SAVE Britain's Heritage, which was eventually to fight a last-ditch battle to stop the Swiss Re tower, was founded in 1975. The year was designated European Architectural Heritage Year, but the demolition of listed buildings was continuing at an alarming rate. Its founding chairman, Marcus Binney, had become well known as a defender of historic country houses, then still a threatened species, but SAVE's attention came to focus on a far wider range of buildings – churches and chapels, industrial monuments, railway stations, barracks and public baths,

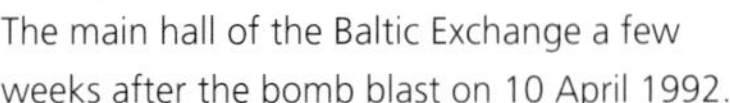

The main hall of the Baltic Exchange a few weeks after the bomb blast on 10 April 1992.

for example. It put new fire into the conservation movement, represented by long-established amenity societies such as the Georgian Group and Victorian Society, and proved adept at getting good publicity for its campaigns: writers and journalists, among them Simon Jenkins, editor successively of the *Evening Standard* and *The Times*, formed a majority of its committee. SAVE was also at pains to point out that the case for preserving old buildings was as much practical as sentimental – they were a resource and could be made to pay. Demolishing them needlessly, it argued, was sheer waste.

The British public, disillusioned by the consequences of much poor new development during the boom in the 1960s, warmed to the message. The title of a SAVE report on the post-war redevelopment of the City of London, *From Splendour to Banality*, said what most people thought. SAVE did not set out to rubbish all modern buildings, but the campaign for 'the heritage' in Britain took on a new dimension in the mid-1980s when the Prince of Wales began to express outspoken views on contemporary architecture. In 1989 the prince lambasted post-war planning in the City. "The London that slowly evolved after the Great Fire took more than three hundred years to build", he wrote. "It took about fifteen years to destroy. What was rebuilt after the war has succeeded in wrecking

London's skyline and spoiling the view of St Paul's in a jostling scrum of skyscrapers, all competing for attention." The prince was opposed to more tall buildings in London, whether or not they were socially and environmentally progressive, and his views, for a time, carried a great deal of weight. One journalist who tended to support his campaigns was Mira Bar-Hillel of the *Evening Standard*. She allegedly "jumped for joy" when she heard that "the window fell out of the Gherkin" in April 2005 (as reported in the *Architects' Journal*, 5 May 2005).

Both English Heritage and the City Corporation maintained their stance on the future of the Baltic Exchange – that reconstruction was the preferred option and demolition was to be resisted for a surprisingly long time. "We were hanging on, despite all the odds, because we'd been told that it *could* be rebuilt", Peter Rees recalls. "But then the alternatives weren't very appealing. Nobody mentioned the possibility of replacing it with a contemporary masterpiece or of a tower with new public space around it. I'm afraid that the Baltic Exchange showed no interest in quality design." Rees points out that the City Corporation held out against demolition until after English Heritage had shifted its position: "once they'd decided that it could go, our position was untenable anyway."

In March 1996 Foster was working on plans for the Millennium Tower, and Trafalgar House (about to be subsumed by Kvaerner) was reportedly talking to a major bank about a possible development on the St Mary Axe site involving an architect of high repute. At this date Paul Drury (who had succeeded Sophie Andreae at English Heritage's London Division) delivered a dramatic report to English Heritage's London Advisory Committee. The interior of the exchange hall had been inspected, he reported, and found to be in a worse condition than expected. (Perhaps this was hardly surprising, since the remains had stood there for four years.) A rebuilding would "be moving much closer to replication than reconstruction". Trafalgar House was, it was alleged, potentially a generous donor to the cause of historic building conservation. If allowed to develop the Baltic Exchange site, it would be prepared to donate a substantial sum, maybe £10 million, towards the repair of other historic City buildings, perhaps some of the numerous churches. (The chairman of English Heritage subsequently denied that any such offer had ever been made.) The committee resolved "that it would be reasonable to consider, in principle, the loss of the remains of the Baltic Exchange in the context of a scheme which provided a new building of high architectural quality".

English Heritage's apparent enthusiasm for new architecture did not extend to the Millennium Tower, which it opposed on the grounds of its potential impact on the London skyline. Nor was there a united view in the organization on the merits of a tall building on the Baltic Exchange site. An officer's report to the London Advisory Committee in February 1999, when the final Swiss Re scheme was about to be submitted for planning permission, recommended that English Heritage oppose the scheme as "unduly dominant and assertive by reason of its

While the Millennium Tower (above) would have been the dominant tower on the city skyline, the newly proposed building (opposite) fits more comfortably into an existing cluster of tall buildings.

height, form, bulk, massing and relationship to nearby high buildings". It would damage the skyline, challenging the dominance of St Paul's, disrupt the setting of nearby listed buildings and impact adversely on the character of the adjacent St Helen's Place conservation area. There was much debate over the report, but in the end the committee rejected its findings and found "the proposed building to be of such exceptional architectural interest that it would be a justifiable replacement for the Baltic Exchange". In due course English Heritage's Commissioners were called on to take a final decision on what was a highly conspicuous project. The "remarkable quality" of Foster's scheme outweighed, they concluded, "the limited adverse impact on the setting of a number of surrounding buildings and areas".

The recommendation, sent to the City Corporation and to the Government Office for London (GOL), was a turning point in the difficult relationship between English Heritage and the cause of new architecture. The election to government in 1997 of the Labour party had brought in an administration apparently suspicious of the 'heritage culture' associated with the political right, and preoccupied with modernizing Britain as well as committed to economic growth. English Heritage was potentially a body at risk of being disbanded. Its support for the 30 St Mary Axe project and for Daniel Libeskind's 'Spiral', first proposed in 1998,

at the Victoria and Albert Museum in South Kensington proved that it could 'move with the times', to the dismay of some conservationists. English Heritage's preoccupation with the perceived threat of tall buildings in London did not, however, go away. Its opposition to the 'Heron Tower' on Bishopsgate, which seemed inconsistent in the light of its support for 30 St Mary Axe, was brushed aside in a ruling by the Secretary of State following a public inquiry. Furthermore, little account was taken of its objections to the proposed 'Shard' in Southwark, south London, which was given consent by Mr Prescott after an extended public inquiry. By backtracking on the approach of his predecessor Sir Jocelyn Stevens and leading English Heritage into a new battle against tall buildings, the organization's chairman, Sir Neil Cossons, seemed to be putting it ever more at odds with the government. English Heritage seemed unaware that the outcome of the Swiss Re saga, to which it had contributed positively, was a watershed for new development in London.

The battle of words over the site and the proposals for its development continued as the prospects for the Millennium Tower faded in 1997. The director of the Victorian Society stated that the society remained "strongly opposed to the demolition of the existing building. Given that it was blown up by the IRA we think it is all the more important that the building is sensitively restored". The sale

The fully restored Baltic Exchange stained-glass windows are now on display at the National Maritime Museum in Greenwich.

of the site to Swiss Re, agreed in late 1997, with the apparent prospect of consent for demolition eventually being given, angered some at the Baltic Exchange. "This is very galling", said its Chief Executive, Jim Buckley, in November 1997. "We will be seeking compensation in the most forcible way possible. We were forced to sell the building cheaply and the price reflected the fact that it had to be restored." (It was reported variously that Swiss Re had paid anything from £80 million to £100 million for the site.) The City Corporation's response was bullish: "they [the Baltic Exchange] should have been more careful in the way they negotiated the sale", a spokesman retorted. The controversy over the City Corporation's and English Heritage's change of direction was to run for several years, and the opponents of the scheme made capital from it. In July 1999 Mira Bar-Hillel argued that, at least, the exchange hall, "one of the most stunning spaces I have ever seen", should be restored, and claimed that the Exchange had been "threatened with prosecution if they did not restore the listed building". It had, she insisted, then been "forced to sell the site for a hugely reduced price on the assumption that the buyer would have to spend some £20 million on the restoration". In the event, the threat of full-scale legal action by the Exchange did not materialize, though it partly underwrote SAVE's attempted judicial review action in autumn 2000.

In fact, great care and considerable funds had been expended on rescuing anything salvageable from the bomb site – up to £4 million was eventually spent on this operation. In late 2000 a special trust was set up, with the City Corporation, English Heritage and Kvaerner (whose responsibility it remained) as members, and a storage site for recovered material found in Essex. Particularly notable, and excluded from the care of the trust, was the series of stained-glass windows of the main staircase that formed the Baltic's memorial to the sixty members who died in the First World War. Designed by J.D. Forsyth and unveiled in 1922, they included panels representing the five Virtues (Hope, Fortitude, Justice, Truth and Faith) set below a glazed dome celebrating the heroism and triumph of war. The glass had been shattered by the explosion, some of the panels being reduced to little more than dust. There was no place to accommodate this memorial in the new Baltic Exchange premises, even if it were to be restored.

Initially, the City Corporation had required that the glass be displayed in a new structure as part of the Swiss Re development, but the Exchange was unhappy with this proposal. In the end, after years of restoration by conservators Goddard & Gibbs, involving replication of destroyed panels on the basis of photographs, the ensemble was installed in the National Maritime Museum at Greenwich, south-east London, with the aid of a grant by Swiss Re. The glass was unveiled there in June 2005. Other materials from the site were offered free of charge to any institutions that would display the materials to the public. But offers were not forthcoming and eventually the materials were passed, as late as February 2003, to an architectural salvage dealer, Derek Davies, who declared that he was ready to sell the lot for £250,000 to anybody willing to reassemble the parts of the building.

Peter Rees of the City Corporation says that he "warmed to the Swiss Re scheme as it developed – the enthusiasm of Swiss Re was very impressive, and infectious". The City Corporation was increasingly aware the building proposed could just be a masterpiece. Positive press comment had come from, among others, the *Evening Standard*'s architecture correspondent, Rowan Moore. Taking a view contrary to that of his colleague Mira Bar-Hillel, Moore commented: "what Sir Norman has now designed is far from being the biggest, but it's the most civilized skyscraper in the world." By this time the proposed Swiss Re tower was already being widely referred to as the 'Gherkin' or (a term that both Norman Foster and his client did not warm to) "the erotic Gherkin". ("Just what *is* an erotic gherkin?" Foster asks.) A refreshingly original view came from the former Victoria and Albert Museum director Sir Roy Strong, who described the proposed building as "a post modern Strawberry Hill … a Gothic skyscraper fantasy that is beguiling and shows up the rubbish that surrounds it. It has elegance and originality".

The campaign to secure planning permission for the building proved to be a long-haul effort despite the involvement of top-notch planning and legal

All five of the Virtues, in this instance Truth, are represented by the figure of a woman. The symbols each have a significance: the mirror represents self-knowledge; the serpent, transformation; the bows and arrows are for communication; and the book denotes wisdom. This window suffered less damage than the other four because it was slightly open at the time of the bombing.

The Baltic Exchange stained glass

The stained glass at the Baltic Exchange was a memorial to the members who gave their lives in the First World War. It was designed by J. Dudley Forsyth, who also has a window in Westminster Abbey, and made by Lowndes and Drury in 1920. The memorial consisted of a half dome and five windows depicting the five Virtues.

A large proportion of the glass was damaged or destroyed by the IRA bomb of April 1992. Those fragments that survived were recovered by craftspeople from Goddard & Gibbs Studios and put into temporary storage. In 1996 the studios produced a full report on the condition of the glass, and in October 2002 Swiss Re instructed Goddard & Gibbs to conserve and restore it so that they could donate it to the National Maritime Museum.

The half dome has a diameter of 8.5 metres, divided into fifteen vertical sections each containing sixteen panels of varying sizes. The five Virtues windows, 1450 x 2160 millimetres overall, depict Justice, Fortitude, Truth, Faith and Hope. The dome had suffered about 40% damage, and some of the Virtues windows more than 70% damage.

Working from existing photographs – there was much better photographic evidence for restoring the centre three Virtues windows (Justice, Fortitude and Truth) than for the two side windows (Hope and Faith) – and using the original glass as a guide, the studios proceeded to restore the glass. The restorers saved as much of the original glass as possible and only painted new pieces if absolutely necessary. All the work was fully documented and the processes used are reversible.

The project was completed in June 2005 and the stained glass is now on display at the National Maritime Museum in Greenwich, London.

Baltic Exchange stained glass in situ in the original hall (photograph c. 1922).

Photograph taken in April 1992 immediately after the April 1992 IRA bombing showing the extent of the damage to the glass.

Studio of J.D. Forsyth, where the glass was designed and manufactured (photograph 1920).

consultants, including Malcolm Kerr and Barnaby Collins, Richard Coleman, a conservation and urban design consultant, and Ray Jackson of the legal firm Linklaters as advisers to Swiss Re. Georgie Gibbs, of Bell Pottinger, a highly experienced and persuasive publicist who had worked with Peter Palumbo on the Number 1 Poultry project, was also a key team member. It was not until May 1999, more than two years after Swiss Re had committed itself to developing the site, that a formal planning application went to the City Corporation. By then, however, negotiations with the City had progressed to the point at which approval could be expected relatively rapidly, while English Heritage had resolved to support the scheme. The application was presented formally to the Corporation's Planning and Transportation Committee on 4 July 2000. The Baltic Exchange was the principal objector, accusing the City Corporation of reversing its previous policy requiring the retention and restoration of the hall. In a letter to committee members Jim Buckley also stressed the broader implications of a decision to approve the scheme. "The new building will have an overpowering visual effect on important listed buildings and surrounding conservation areas", he argued. Buckley also suggested that the building would have a detrimental effect on views of the Tower of London, a World Heritage Site. Peter Rees's report was unequivocal in its recommendation to the committee to back the scheme, both for its outstanding quality and for its contribution to the standing of the City as a world financial centre. The report was not rubber-stamped; in fact there was an extended debate on the application, with the members eventually approving it by eighteen votes to seven. On 20 July the Corporation's Court of Common Council formally endorsed the committee's decision. There was jubilation at Swiss Re when the decision emerged – the champagne flowed freely.

In 1999 the project was publicly exhibited in a temporary pavilion on the site as part of the planning process.

Louis Hellman's cartoon, published in the *Architects' Journal*, 28 September 2000, characteristically lampoons the planning debate over the project.

SAVE'S LEGAL CHALLENGE

SAVE's legal challenge, launched in October 2000 after the City Corporation had resolved to grant planning and listed building consent, came as a shock. The aim was to force the Secretary of State, John Prescott, to hold a full public inquiry into the demolition and redevelopment plans. "We thought we were there, planning to get started, and then – boom! – the whole thing's back into the courts", Sara Fox, Swiss Re's Project Director in London, recalls. In fact, Prescott had already reviewed the arguments for and against the development. In February 2000 he had imposed a 'stop notice' on the planning process and he subsequently demanded that an environmental impact assessment (EIA) of the project be carried out in view of its "significant effects on the environment because of its nature, size and location". Swiss Re, though publicly "extremely surprised and disappointed", was well prepared for such a demand, though the City Corporation expressed its frustration with the Secretary of State's intervention. Graham Forbes, the Deputy Chairman of its Planning and Transportation Committee, was critical of the impact of "an additional layer of bureaucracy" that could "inhibit the ongoing redevelopment and regeneration of the City necessary to keep it at the leading edge of world finance". When the City Corporation had refused to order an EIA, the Baltic Exchange had threatened legal action to compel it to do so. The issuing of the EIA was the first time that this provision, an innovation stemming from European Union (EU) directives, had been used in the City, and there was concern in property industry circles about its potential impact. Although the project team was faced with a substantial task in producing the report – a document of considerable bulk – it was accepted by the GOL, opening the way

The complex geometry of Norman Foster's Great Court roof at the British Museum has clear parallels with the glazing of 30 St Mary Axe.

for Prescott to approve the scheme. English Heritage's London Advisory Committee had accepted the findings of the EIA in June 2000, setting aside a number of objections. (Among these was one, focusing on distant views of the tower, from a former City planner, Anthony Tugnutt, whose subsequent opposition to Foster's British Museum Great Court scheme was rooted in a similar townscape analysis.) The confirmation of Prescott's decision came in a letter from the GOL, dated 23 August 2000. There was to be no public inquiry and the City Corporation's decision was to be the last word.

This was an outcome that neither the Baltic Exchange nor SAVE was prepared to accept. Jim Buckley promised that the Exchange would support SAVE financially with its proposed application for a process of judicial review. This would empower senior judges to scrutinize the Secretary of State's decision and possibly to decide that it was improper, in which case a public inquiry would be unavoidable. "The proper way for us to deal with this is to ensure that SAVE has got enough funds, so we'll match what they raise, pound for pound", Buckley told the press early in October 2000. SAVE's secretary, Richard Pollard, was adamant that "the City's planning officer, the conservation specialists who oversaw the dismantling of the building in 1996 and even the applicant all agree that it would be possible to restore the Baltic Exchange hall"; the case for a 'call in', as the legal process is known, was irrefutable, he contended. Judicial review is an uncertain and potentially very costly business. Before this review could even be set in motion, SAVE's lawyers had to convince a judge that there was a substantial case to be addressed, which would thereby enable them to obtain the necessary 'leave' to seek judicial review. The machinery was designed to filter out objections that were ill-founded or purely vexatious.

Irritating as SAVE's challenge was to Swiss Re and the City Corporation, it was both sincerely motivated – the organization's commitment to conserving historic buildings was not in doubt – and rooted in an interpretation of the legislation that held some weight. It could not be taken lightly.

SAVE abandoned its legal action after papers from the office of the Treasury Solicitor were delivered to the High Court on the eve of the formal hearing. The document explained the series of decisions made by Mr Prescott and the way in which he had measured them against the provisions of PPG15. "The Secretary of State recognizes that the development proposals in this case could be regarded as falling within the scope of his policy of call in for applications for listed building consent", it stated. The Secretary of State, it continued, had decided that "the circumstances of the case did not lead him to conclude that the application should be called in", especially when he took into account English Heritage's advice on the matter. To continue with the case would have meant challenging the Secretary of State's wide discretionary powers. Had SAVE lost, it would have faced substantial costs that could have triggered its bankruptcy, so the action was withdrawn. SAVE commented that the case "sends out a message that if a developer lobbies hard and high enough and finds a prestigious enough architect then they can secure the demolition of a listed building, regardless of guidance and legislation". Mira Bar-Hillel of the *Evening Standard*, a tireless opponent of the project, thundered that a "stunning" listed building that had "survived" the bombing in 1992 – a questionable assertion – was to be destroyed. "Small wonder that SAVE are now concerned for the future of all our historic buildings, which appear to have no champion any more", she concluded. Marcus Binney believes that SAVE was right to pursue the action. "There was no evidence that the Secretary of State had seriously considered the case", he says. "We finally got confirmation that he had – that was important. The action did reinforce the workings of the legislation even if it didn't save the building."

Overleaf
A model of the City, commissioned by the City Corporation, shows projects both completed and proposed.

Today, the Baltic Exchange is a largely forgotten City structure, a relatively modest loss in a toll that includes far better buildings, while London has gained a contemporary landmark that is known the world over. But for the heinous action of terrorists, no proposal to demolish the Exchange could ever have succeeded. But many will conclude that Norman Foster's remarkable tower is preferable to a patched-up replica of a historic building and that the 'save the Baltic Exchange' campaign ended up as a rather irrational crusade against the inevitable. For Peter Wynne Rees of the City Corporation, 30 St Mary Axe has "changed the public perception of tall buildings single-handedly. People come up to me and say how great it is. I'm waiting for someone to demand that the setting of 30 St Mary Axe be protected like that of St Paul's!"

Negative media comment on the project had been more than balanced by favourable accounts. Martin Pawley, one of the few critics to support strongly the Millennium Tower project, had attacked the "fogeys" who opposed the Swiss Re tower. The Baltic Exchange was not a splendid historic building, as they claimed, but "a collection of numbered bits". Rowan Moore felt that the building "could be exactly the inspiring tower we lack" (*Evening Standard*, 12 April 2000). The tower "will have the quality of Foster's best work, which is that there is nothing that is lazily conventional, but everything is considered and thought through. The client is not some chancer developer, but an insurance company building for its own use, with a record of building well", Moore commented. Hugh Pearman of the *Sunday Times* was also positive, as was *The Observer*'s Deyan Sudjic. Jonathan Glancey, writing in *The Guardian* in the spring of 2001, anticipated "a very special building where the latest in computer-aided design has been matched to an acute environmental awareness". He looked forward to the building's completion: "Will we learn to love it? Let's hope so. But what we must do is learn to demand that any new tall building in our city centres be as painstakingly and imaginatively designed as this." Among critics attached to the national daily press, only Marcus Binney – by then SAVE's President – was less than enthusiastic, focusing less on the building than on the skyline issues that tall buildings in general raised and attacking Ken Livingstone's support for them. Even Binney, however, had to admit that "it will be an eye-catching addition to the City skyline, bringing much-needed interest to the dull cluster of existing blocks" (*The Times*, 23 July 1999). In a pompous editorial on 8 May 2001 *The Times* raised the absurd spectre of "perpetual twilight" being cast on the area around "the gherkin". The Tower of Babel had fallen and "bad times have dogged big towers ever since", it suggested.

On 11 September 2001 an event took place that appeared to prove *The Times* right and which certainly threatened to set back the cause of high buildings. The terrorist attack on the twin towers of Manhattan's World Trade Center, resulting in terrible loss of life, gave fuel to the 'antis'. The St Mary Axe project was, however, already on site: it could not be abandoned without massive cost. "We

The ceremony on 12 October 2001 marked the official 'start of steel' on site.

had finished the piling and poured the concrete for the basement, eleven hours when a constant stream of trucks delivered concrete to the site", Sara Fox recalls. The team reeled at the horror of what had happened, then got on with the job in hand. It was a month later, on 12 October, that a symbolic 'ground-breaking' event was held. In fact, the ground had already been 'broken' so this was a 'start of steel' ceremony, in which the first of the great A-frames in the building was raised. Swiss Re's chairman, Peter Forstmoser, spoke and confronted the issue of '9/11' head on. There was no way back and the project proceeded.

DEVELOPING THE DESIGN

DEVELOPING THE DESIGN

Most of the models constructed during the design process were made in-house by the design team.

An exhibition in 2001 at the Louisiana Museum of Modern Art in Denmark brought together many of the working models for the project.

INITIAL STAGES

Few new London buildings in recent years have aroused the degree of public interest that 30 St Mary Axe generated even before its construction had begun. Not surprisingly perhaps, the public's view of the building has been, at times, distorted: the project has spawned more than its fair share of speculation, hearsay and myth, including extraordinary reports that the tower was "sinking into the ground" during construction. 'Iconic' buildings – a description often applied to 30 St Mary Axe – tend to give rise to such stories.

Robin Partington, the Foster and Partners director (who has since left the practice) responsible for developing the designs and then turning a series of ideas into a building, tackles one of those myths head-on. "The building was not, as many imagine, designed using computer programs", he insists. "This was an analogue building, you could say. There was no magic 'eureka' moment, no blinding flash of inspiration when the form of the building suddenly became fixed. It was more a matter of bloody hard work. In the Foster office, good ideas are ten a penny." Partington singles out Ian Bogle and Jason Parker for their skill with foamboard and coloured pencils, and Julian Cross for his visualizations of the building in context. "The real skill", Partington says, "lies in sorting them out, picking out the ones that work, testing and tuning the concept – and then getting it built." In short, it is a matter of the proverbial 1% inspiration and 99% perspiration, though that 1% inspiration is what makes the project remarkable. Nor does Partington have any patience with suggestions that there is some mystical idea at the heart of the design – the Fibonacci sequence (a sequence of numbers in which each is the sum of the two preceding ones), for example – or the inspiration of an object in nature. (The critic Charles Jencks has described the building as a "cosmic dome".) "It was more about lots of cardboard and plastic. We didn't have the computer skills [in the late 1990s] then to work out the design that way – instead,

Foster and Partners' riverside studio in Battersea, London.

we made hundreds and hundreds of models, small and large. The computer came into its own when we had to work out a way of building the final design." Stuart Milne's CAD co-ordination was crucial at this stage, and Hugh Whitehead and Francis Aish used parametric modelling to develop the building's design.

Foster and Partners is a large practice by global, let alone London, standards. Norman Foster heads a team of around six hundred people, assisted by a group of directors, some of whom have been colleagues since the days of the Hongkong Bank. The notion that Foster personally designed 30 St Mary Axe at a time when scores of other major projects were being tackled by his office is patently absurd. Yet it was Foster's vision that drove the project, and the teamwork that is fundamental to his practice's phenomenal success that got it built. It was Norman Foster who had 'reinvented' the tall office building, in Hong Kong, and even before that created a workplace for Willis Faber & Dumas in Ipswich that remains radical even

The variety of models ranged from conceptual form-making (right) to detailed structures examining the resolution of the top of the tower (top) and different patterns of atria (above).

today. The social dimension of design remains a driving force for Foster's architecture, and that social vision is in tune with new thinking about the office in which social activity and interaction are key objectives. Foster is equally preoccupied by the environmental issues surrounding building design. He looks back to his work with the truly visionary designer Buckminster Fuller and the latter's pursuit of a benign technology that would serve humanity without damaging the natural world. The Duisburg projects had seen that vision translated into real buildings, and the lessons learned fed into the revolutionary Commerzbank tower.

Foster believes that 30 St Mary Axe is a truly radical building, certainly in the context of the world of business. And while he pays tribute to the vision of his clients at Swiss Re – "the biggest act of faith was the decision to commission the building in the first place" – he argues that one of the duties of the architect is to be the advocate of new ideas, rejecting the time-worn and the obvious. Foster had to fight for the idea of a dome on the Berlin Reichstag: "people said nobody would want to go up there, even if it was sensible to let them, and that the restaurant wouldn't pay its way. Now it's the most popular in Germany!" It was his advocacy, along with the commitment of his client, that ensured that the radical ideas in 30 St Mary Axe were not watered down in the long process of planning, design and construction.

Late in 1997, with the Millennium Tower project, even in its reduced version, effectively dead – and Norman Foster still believes that the revised scheme could have been built – the Foster team explored possible alternative strategies for the

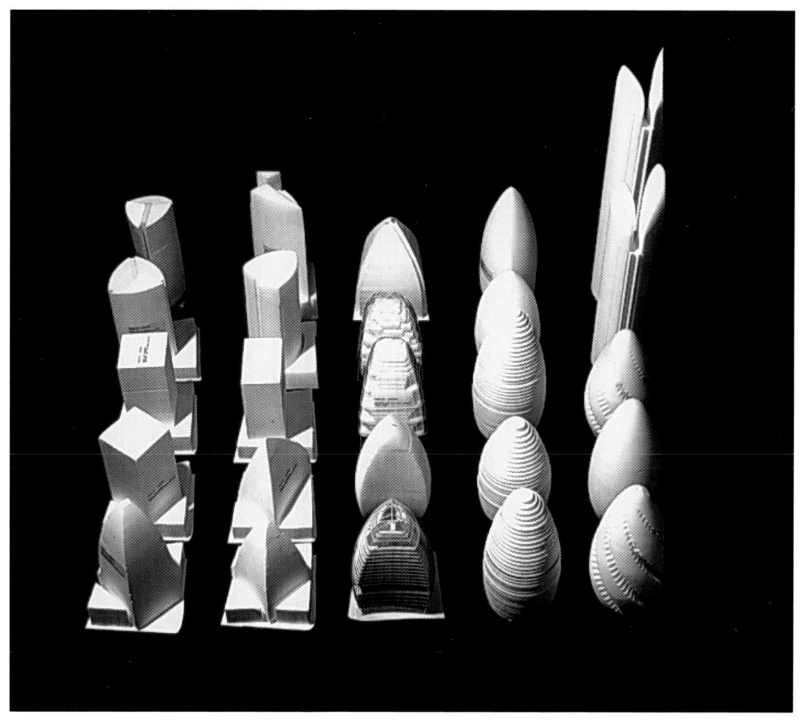

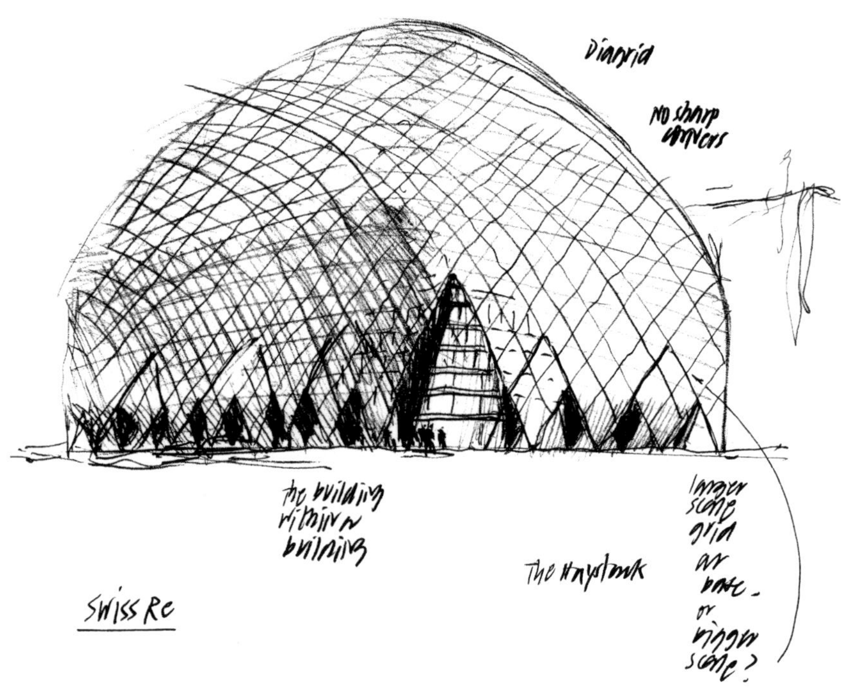

One of Norman Foster's early ideas for the site took the form of a 'haystack' with an organic structure that lent itself to the concept of a 'building within a building'. This idea developed into the final form of the building (opposite).

Baltic Exchange site. At this stage the team included Ken Shuttleworth, who had worked with Norman Foster on the Millennium Tower. Both Foster and Shuttleworth are in the habit of sketching constantly, producing a flood of ideas; Shuttleworth, as he admits, is after all imbued with the creative ethos of the Foster office. Initially the emphasis was on a substantially lower building, and during late 1997 the scheme variously nicknamed the 'haystack', 'beehive' or 'loaf of bread', filling the whole site and providing around 530,000 square feet (49,290 square metres) net of usable space within a building with a height of 110 metres was briefly on offer, the developer's aim being to attract an appropriate City institution as the tenant. Swiss Re, which was actively searching for a building – it looked at more than thirty possible locations – was one potential taker. But it was not until the very end of 1997 that the company came to an agreement with Kvaerner that it would acquire the St Mary Axe site, subject to planning permission being obtained, and develop a bespoke London headquarters there.

By February of the following year a concept design for Swiss Re had been developed by Foster. It provided for a very large building, at 130 metres significantly shorter than what was eventually built but with deep floors giving it a girth that some felt was ungainly. English Heritage, which was warming to the idea of a new building of high quality finally replacing the battered remains of the Baltic Exchange, commented that it was too bulky. The City Corporation, which was shown the scheme in this month, was equivocal, suggesting that it be evaluated against the GMW groundscraper scheme (for which planning consent already

5
a reflective
solar top
following
the 'o'
shading..
The
'maypole'
effect?
The
city
grid
The "city grid" is
really a 4-storey
increment, visually
NF
The "city within a city" has
always been full of surprises!

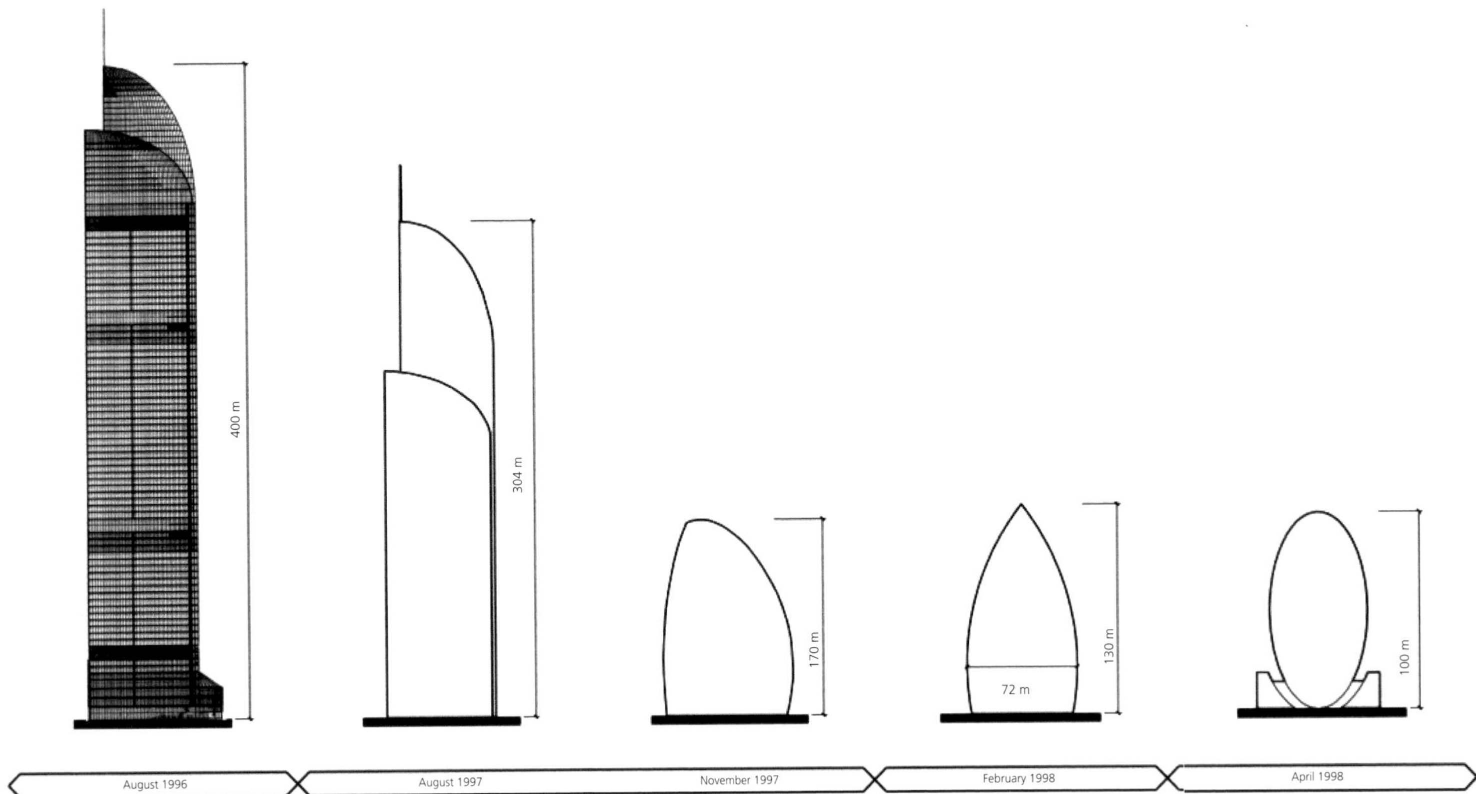

1,607,060 sq ft net floor area above ground level.

Planning Application withdrawn February 1998.

1,091,968 sq ft net floor area above ground level.

A reduced-height version of the London Millennium Tower (LMT).

Not the subject of a planning application.

537,742 sq ft net floor area above ground level.

A further reduction in height but the individual floor plates are larger than those of the LMT.

Proposals offered to potential City occupiers.

600,000 sq ft net floor area above ground level.

Proposal presented to the Corporation of London planners 12 February 1998, who commented that:

- The concept was of interest but could be regarded by some as alien within the City of London.
- The design did not address the issues raised by English Heritage in a letter of 22 March 1996 (in relation to the GMW scheme), regarding the perceived bulk of the building and the importance of replacing the Baltic Exchange with a building of architectural merit and designed by an architect of repute.
- An analysis of the GMW scheme was recommended to establish a total net floor area above ground level as a basis for further discussion.

Proposal presented to English Heritage 25 February 1998, who commented that the perceived bulk of the building, as stated in their letter of 22 March 1996, should be minimized within the design.

600,000 sq ft net floor area above ground level.

Proposal presented to English Heritage 6 April 1998, who commented that:

- Inclusion of the podium left the issues of architectural merit and perceived bulk unresolved.
- The amount of floor area above ground level was considered excessive for the site although a taller building may be more appropriate.
- A taller building may be appropriate on this site.

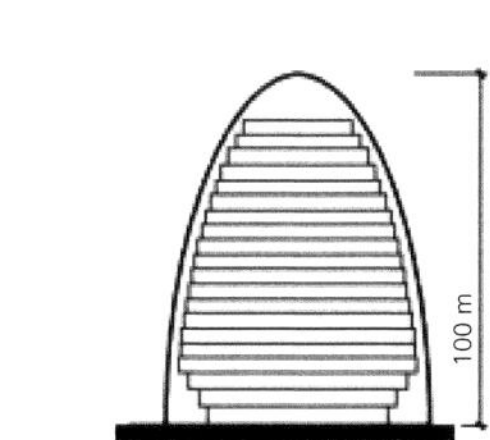

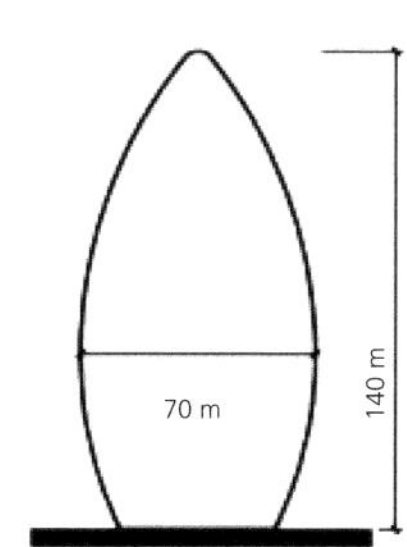

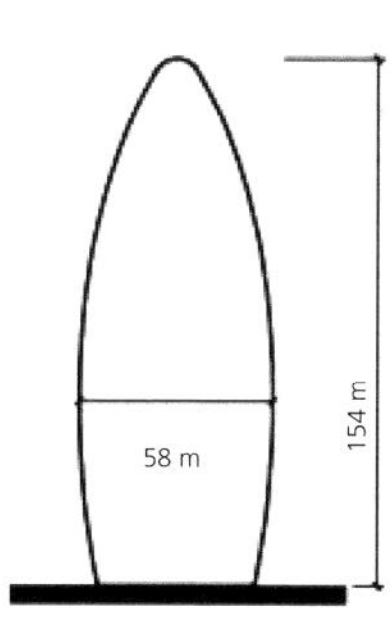

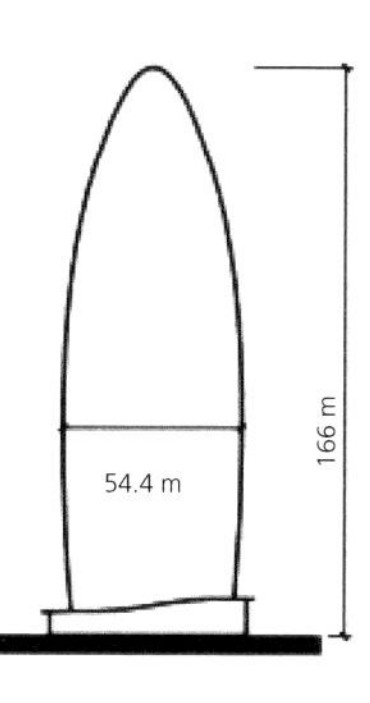

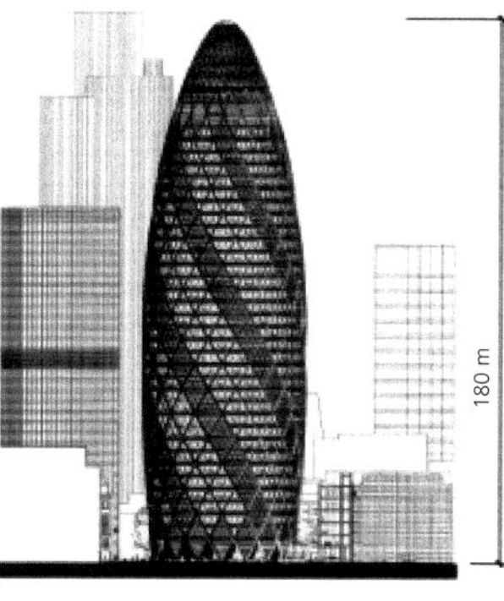

May–July 1998 | August 1998 | October 1998 | October 1998–February 1999 | July 1999

Design Development with Corporation of London and English Heritage

Planning Application

500,000 sq ft net floor area above ground level.

Tower and podium configuration amended to strengthen the architectural concept of a 'building within a building'.

The design responded to English Heritage comments in respect of architectural merit and perceived bulk, through its curved form.

500,000 sq ft net floor area above ground level.

The tower is set within a plaza to contribute to the City environment and create an appropriate setting for adjacent buildings.

It encompasses further response to English Heritage comments in respect of perceived bulk and architectural merit.

Proposals were presented to Corporation of London planners 13 August 1998, who commented that the tower proportions were too bulky at its girth and the net floor area above ground level was excessive.

450,000 sq ft net floor area above ground level.

The proposal was presented to Corporation of London planners 19 and 21 October 1998 who commented that:

- The tower proportions remained too bulky at its girth, but a further increase in height might be appropriate.
- Net floor area above ground level was considered acceptable.
- The public realm configuration around the base of the building was a cause for concern. The introduction of perimeter buildings to shield exposed gable walls and offer accommodation open to the public was recommended.

Height of tower was increased and width reduced to improve the building's proportions.

450,000 sq ft net floor area above ground level.

Perimeter buildings containing accommodation accessible by the public on the northern and eastern edges of the site were proposed to maintain the streetscape.

The open plaza area on the southern and western edges was maintained to allow views from the building's entrance.

Proposal presented to Corporation of London planners 28 October, 5 November and18 November 1998, who commented that the height of the tower should be further increased and the girth should be reduced to achieve proportions they considered acceptable.

Proposals presented to Corporation of London planners, English Heritage and the Royal Fine Art Commission (RFAC) 1, 14 and 15 December 1998, and 18 January and 10 February 1999.

- The Corporation of London planners and the RFAC confirmed that they considered the building satisfactory on the City skyline despite reservations expressed by English Heritage officers.
- English Heritage and the RFAC identified that further design development was required in respect of the perimeter buildings and improvement in the quality of the public realm at the base of building.

450,000 sq ft net floor area above ground level.

The Royal Fine Art Commission confirmed acceptance of the scheme as an appropriate tall building for the City of London in a letter dated 16 February 1999, although it recommended a further increase in the height of the building to improve elegance.

A letter from English Heritage dated 22 March 1999 confirmed the proposal to be of appropriate quality to replace the Baltic Exchange, but recommended the omission of the perimeter building to improve the building's setting.

Revised proposals presented to Corporation of London planners, English Heritage and the RFAC on 6 May and 1 June 1999. The key points were as follows:

- The entire double-height ground floor, with the exception of the building's entrance, should be devoted to 'Class A' type uses.
- A building at the corner of Bury Street and Burt Court, with 'Class A' type uses at ground level and on the first floor, was considered acceptable to terminate the vehicular ramp and exposed gable wall.
- Low-level walls were considered acceptable to define the streetscape.
- Retail kiosks (subsequently deleted) and groups of trees at each corner of the site were considered appropriate elements to enliven the plaza area and to respond to the urban context, in particular the change in direction of St Mary Axe at the north-west corner.

Planning permission granted in July 2000.

Early sketches submitted as part of the planning process show the plaza at the base of the tower as a permeable public space replacing the solid mass of buildings that previously filled the area.

existed), though there was no suggestion that Swiss Re would be interested in developing and occupying a building of the latter type. The only positive aspect of the GMW scheme, from the point of view of the City Corporation and English Heritage, was that it incorporated part of the Baltic Exchange, the battle over the demolition of which still presented a major obstacle to the development of the site.

Behind the scenes City planning chief Peter Rees was holding regular meetings with the Foster team. "He was finding his way in the project and really trying to get the right solution", Robin Partington recalls. "He contributed actively to the development of the scheme." Swiss Re's collaboration with Foster was already producing innovative ideas. The company, with its firm commitment to sustainability, was extremely interested in the notion of an environmentally progressive building in the mould of the Frankfurt Commerzbank. The Foster team was simultaneously looking further at the possibilities of the landlocked City site. It would be possible, they believed, to create a new public realm around the building, opening up new pedestrian routes where none had hitherto existed. The idea of a circular, relatively tall building would allow much of the site to become public space, though the example of the CU plaza of the 1960s, just across the street, provided an object lesson in the mistakes of the past. Generous in scale, it was a place of passage where no one lingered, not least because the winds generated by the tower made it an inhospitable place.

THE FINAL FORM

The final form of the tower was far from being a matter of chance or a mere whim of the architect; it was a response to the environmental and urban issues that drove the project. By the spring of 1998 the building had assumed an egg-like shape, providing a variety of floor plate sizes and a total of around 600,000 square feet (55,800 square metres) of usable space. The 'egg' would sit rather awkwardly on a podium, containing retail space, a device that was soon abandoned. Working with the City Corporation and within the evolving guidelines laid down by English Heritage, the Foster team thought again. There were interesting reflections both of Foster's and Buckminster Fuller's Climatroffice project (1971) and of Willis Faber in the proposal for a 'building within a building' with an intermediate environmental zone between the outer skin and the office floors that could have important implications in terms of energy use. It was in May 1998 that a hint of the final form the building would take emerged. Sketches done at that time showed a circular tower that extended outwards from its base (kept small to maximize the public space around it) then tapered slightly at the crown. The City Corporation's reservations still seemed to focus on the bulk of the building: it wanted to know how much of it would actually be occupied by Swiss Re and how much let. For Carla Picardi and the project team this process was frustrating: London was being offered a world-class building. What concern was it of the City Corporation who was to occupy it? But underlying the Corporation's rigorous analysis of the scheme was, of course, the fact that Peter Rees and the members of the Planning and Transportation Committee were under pressure from a conservationist lobby bent on stopping Foster and from those concerned about the impact of a new tower on City views.

It would be wrong, however, to see the planning process, extended as it was, as simply a matter of delay and compromise. As Sara Fox confirms, the period of nearly two years in which the applications for planning and listed building consent were being prepared and processed was also a time during which the scheme could be developed in detail, ready for tendering, so that when consent was finally given it would be possible to start construction promptly. During the course of 1998–99 the scheme developed in line with the City Corporation's prescriptions on the size of the new building; around 450,000 square feet (41,850 square metres) net was judged acceptable, a reduction of 25% on the initial Foster proposals. The height of the tower increased steadily, from 154 metres to 166 metres and finally 180 metres (590 feet), greatly improving its proportions. The City Corporation's backing for a redesign in this direction was supported by the RFAC, which was not "persuaded that the form of the building had yet achieved an elegance equal to the technical ingenuity it embodied. There was a dumpiness about the proportions which might, in the Commission's view, be remedied by a slightly taller, slimmer profile."

Foster and colleagues were not used to being told by planners that a building should be a little *taller*, but the recommendation was received and acted upon: the tower gained three extra floors. There was never an intention on the part of either architect or client to make the building the tallest in the City, though; it was the bulk, rather than the height, of the tower that had worried the planners. Norman Foster feels, however, that this was a wise move, given the lobby against tall buildings in London. "In any other great world city, we would have said: go for the top, build the tallest building yet seen there. Not in London – Swiss Re got built because it was a little lower than Tower 42." Walter Kielholz of Swiss Re confirms that "our idea was never to build the tallest building in London – the final height was actually set by the planners".

The RFAC also considered that more thought needed to be given to the new public space around the building and its relationship to surrounding buildings and streets. This was an issue on which the City Corporation deliberated at length. The 0.57 hectare site had been created by, in effect, an act of war. In this way it resembled some of the City sites opened up by Second World War bombs, with the gables of adjacent buildings rawly exposed. To the east, on Bury Street, the site faced a major listed building, H.P. Berlage's Holland House (1914–16), a unique British work by this great Dutch architect. The townscape of Bury Street had been shattered by the bomb in 1992, and the planners looked at ways in

The context of the tower includes a major listed building by Dutch architect H.P. Berlage, Holland House (1914–16).

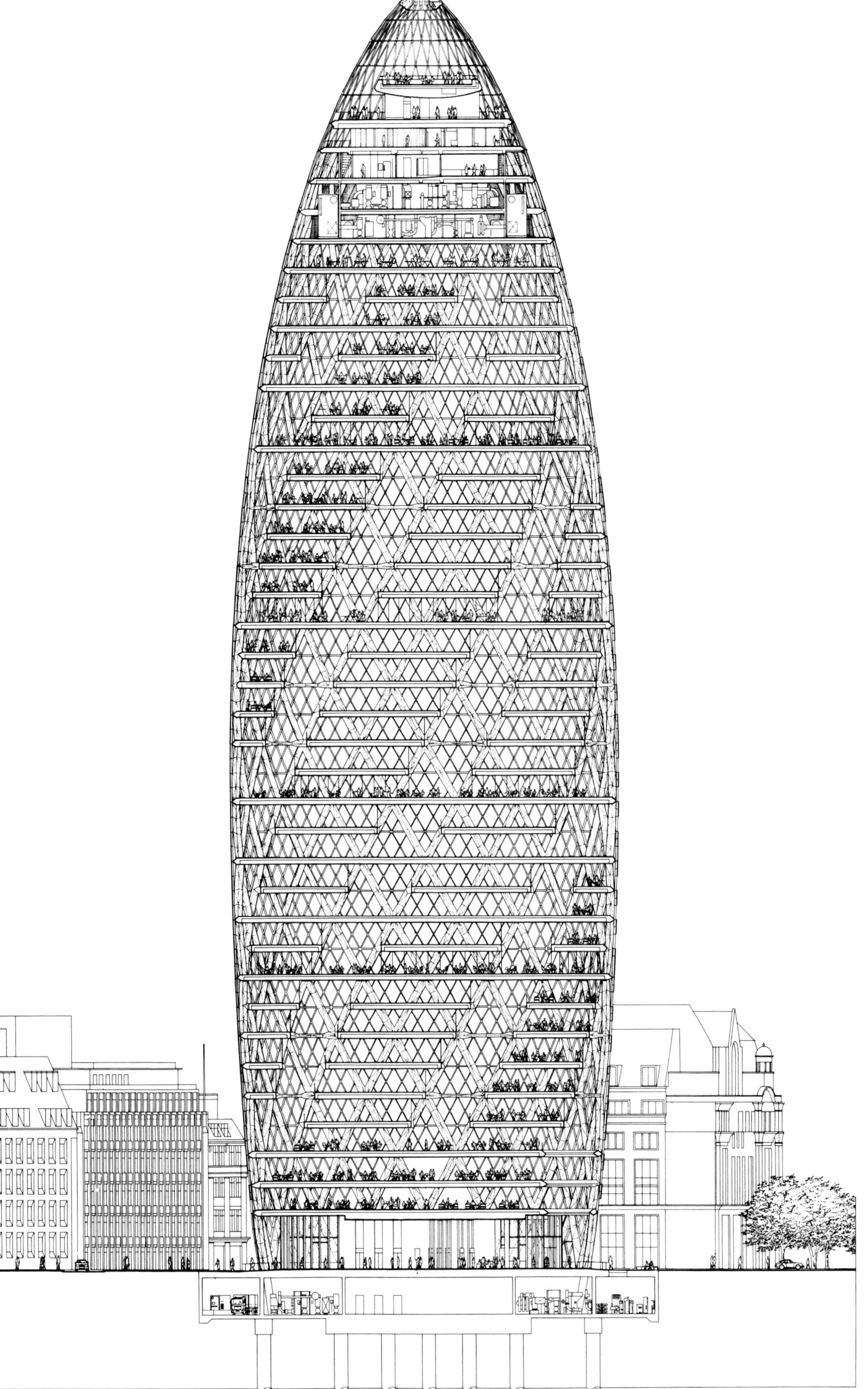

LEVEL 40 (diameter 22 metres):
The bar area at the summit of the building showing the circular staircase giving access to this level with a platform lift at its centre.

LEVEL 39 (diameter 27 metres):
The restaurant level also has to accommodate kitchens, WCs, lifts, escape stairs and services.

LEVEL 33 (diameter 43 metres):
This reflected ceiling plan shows the radial layout typical of floors 28–34, which do not have triangular atria.

LEVEL 21 (diameter 56 metres):
A typical office floor on the mid-rise lift bank. Note the six triangular atria creating orthogonal 'fingers' of floorspace.

LEVEL 6 (diameter 54 metres):
A typical office floor on the low-rise lift bank.

ENTRANCE LEVEL (diameter 49 metres):
The west-facing entrance lobby gives access to three sets of lift banks: low-, medium- and high-rise. Space to the east is allocated for retail use.

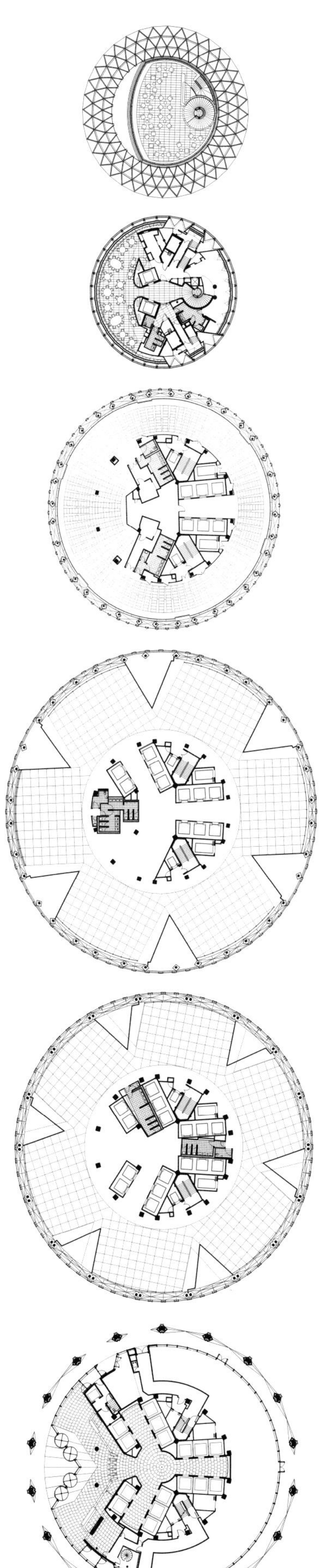

Opposite
Section through the building, including basement level (Drawing: Birds Portchmouth Russum Architects).

which it could be repaired. There were suggestions that a high wall or even a colonnade could be built along Bury Street to contain the Swiss Re site, though the City Corporation eventually relaxed its stance. Low stone walls doubling up as benches were substituted, along with trees; the space was kept clear of the clutter that spoils so many public squares in Britain. An idea that a substantial structure some 8 metres high would be built on the new plaza to house the Baltic Exchange stained glass was also abandoned. (Instead it went to the National Maritime Museum at Greenwich.)

The plaza was regarded, reasonably enough, as a public benefit that the developer would provide in return for consent to erect a tall building. The juxtaposition of a circular building, which has a diameter of just 49 metres at its base, with a roughly rectangular site created spaces of an 'organic', irregular character that now seem far more in tune with London than the Manhattan-style CU plaza. "The 'city within a city' has always been full of surprises", Norman Foster commented. Shops and cafes at the ground level of the tower and in the small building that sits to the north, over the ramp to the basement parking and services area, animate the area around the building. (A suggestion that retailing be extended down into basement areas was rejected by Swiss Re.) It is hard to imagine this as the interior of a built-up City block.

Circular office buildings are a rare breed, for obvious reasons. The working spaces they contain tend to be awkwardly shaped and therefore are potentially

The triangular stepped atria – six per floor – convert each circular floorplate into a series of rectangular spaces.

Spatial accessibility

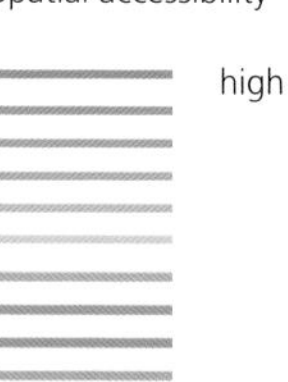

As part of the planning process a detailed analysis of pedestrian traffic was commissioned, revealing the potential for new routes across the proposed plaza.

difficult to let. Foster's strategy was to combine the circular form with rectangular office floors, creating six 'fingers' of space radiating out from a central service core containing lifts, stairs, washrooms and service risers. These fingers could be reduced in size as the building tapered inwards towards its base and top. The aim of such a design was to maximize daylight penetration into the building and to optimize the views out from the office floors, which would themselves be of a relatively conventional format. The maximum distance from core to inner façade in the completed building is 14 metres. The triangular spaces created between the fingers would extend virtually the full height of the building and would be a key element in a low-energy ventilation strategy. At first, these spaces were envisaged as straight lines down the tower, producing vertiginous and slightly threatening chasms. By rotating the floors by 5 degrees at each level in succession, to form stepped atria rising up the building, a more dynamic effect could be obtained. The new diagram was developed in the Foster office using a series of models. According to Paul Scott, a member of the Foster team who later worked with Glenn Howells Architects, "we developed the architecture first, then set about making it work practically. There was a certain amount of post-rationalization". The design process was, according to Sara Fox, "untidy but really creative". Fox sat in on many sessions as the ideas for the building were hammered out.

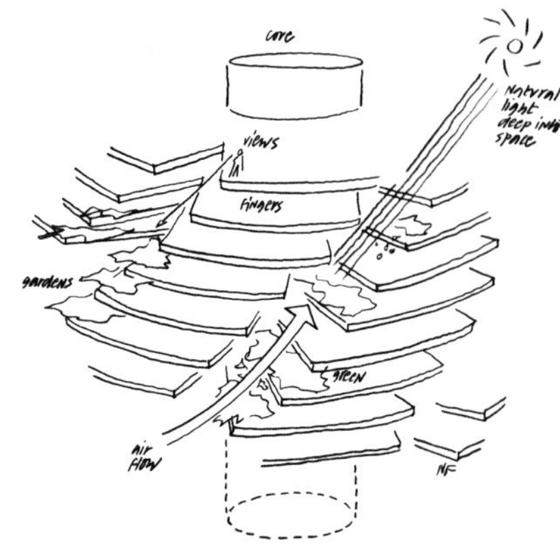

Foster's initial proposal to rotate the atria anti-clockwise was reversed to maximize the potential for ventilation from the prevailing south-west winds.

Both the circular form and the stepped, spiralling atria worked extremely well when it came to realizing the natural ventilation programme for the building, although they both originated in an essentially architectural re-evaluation of the designs. Swiss Re was committed to an 'environmentally progressive' scheme, but that term was not precisely defined at the start of the project. Paul Scott, who took over as project director after Robin Partington's departure from the practice, had worked with Partington on the Commerzbank and Foster's later ARAG Headquarters in Düsseldorf, both extremely progressive in environmental terms. "But the City of London was different: there was always the likelihood that some of the space would be let to tenants", says Scott. "Given the office culture of London, somewhere between that of Europe and North America, there had to be an element of choice. So there was conventional air conditioning alongside natural ventilation. The building was to be highly progressive for London – that didn't necessarily mean embracing standards that would be acceptable in, say, Zurich or Frankfurt." One requirement that the Foster team had to consider was that of fire safety – always to the fore in tall building projects. There had to be provision to extract smoke rapidly from the atria should there be a fire, which meant incorporating opening vents. The vents could be used for other purposes: they were developed as opening windows that brought fresh air into the building. The same fire safety provisions meant that the voids were formed as stacks of floors, each stack being six storeys high. These manageable compartments could be closed down and dealt with in the event of a fire, which could thereby be contained and prevented from spreading up or down the tower.

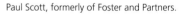

Paul Scott, formerly of Foster and Partners.

Like the Commerzbank gardens, the ARAG building in Düsseldorf incorporates enclosed gardens separated from the office space.

The spiralling atria were practical components in the operational and environmental programme for the building, drawing in and circulating fresh air by means of the positive and negative pressures generated by the geometry of the tower. Dominic Munro of the leading engineering practice Arup, which acted as project structural engineer for Swiss Re under director John Brazier, understood Foster's wish to give the building a dynamic 'push', supplied by the spirals, "but the natural ventilation angle came later", he says. The designs were to provide a serious challenge for Arup. (The practice, under Anthony Ferguson, was also appointed as consultant for the fire engineering design.)

For Norman Foster, the spiralling atria had another potential dimension, as gardens in the sky. "Compared to the typical tall building, Swiss Re, I believed, would be like comparing a ride in a sports car to that in a conventional saloon", he says. "It would offer a new view of the world." The atria in the building were the key to its transparency and its radicalism in so many respects. But they did not become the sky gardens that he envisaged, as planted spaces recalling those in the Commerzbank. As in the case of the Hongkong and Shanghai Bank, the client was not convinced and Foster remains disappointed at what he sees as a failure to realize the full potential of the spaces. "I think there was a point when the Rottweilers were let loose on the scheme", he says. "The big picture, a radical, ground-breaking building, remains, but this is one area where we lost the argument." Paul Scott recalls "recurring disagreements" over the issue. "In my view,

Sustainable design

The low-energy ventilation strategy for 30 St Mary Axe reflected Swiss Re's aspiration to make the building an exemplar of environmentally friendly design. The environmental concept for the tower was developed in tandem with the parametric modelling of its structural form.

The advantages of the curvaceous form were, in this respect, considerable. Instead of wind forces being pushed downwards, as in the rectangular high-rises of an earlier generation, wind would flow around the tower, producing positive pressures on the windward aspect with negative pressures on the sides of the building, a perfect driving force for cross-flow natural ventilation. External air is drawn into the building through motorized perimeter windows placed in each atrium, which also act as intermediate buffer zones to protect office spaces from excessive draughts. The building is equipped for mixed-mode ventilation: conventional air conditioning is available when external conditions make it impractical to open the windows. The top three floors of the building, which are not connected to the lightwells, are entirely air conditioned.

The low-energy strategy was pursued equally in the design of the active, ventilated façade, comprising a low-emissivity double-glazed clear unit on the outside and a single layer of glass on the inside, separated by a cavity between 1 metre and 1.4 metres in depth. Extracted air from the office spaces is passed through the cavity, which also takes heat reflected by metallic-

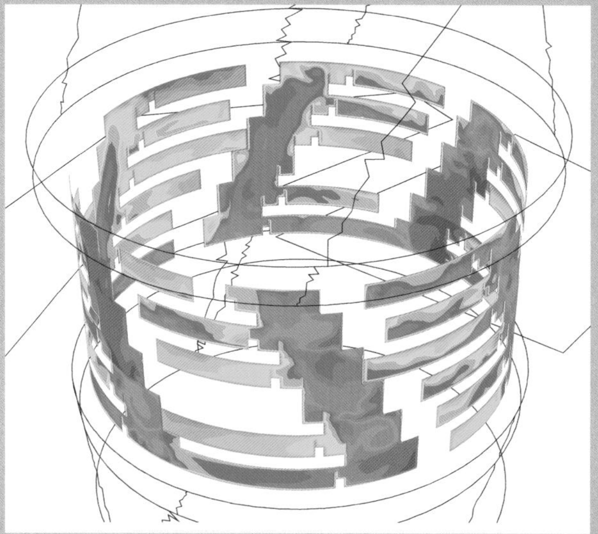

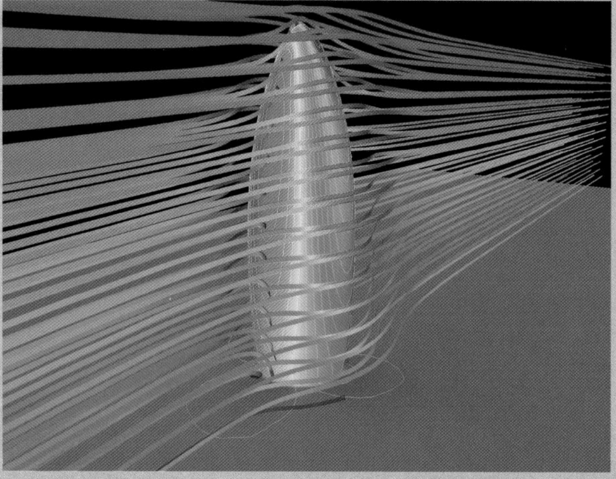

Hilson Moran's team used computer modelling to test the speed of air movement across a typical office floor when the windows are open (top), the temperature on the exterior of the building when vents are open (centre), and the wind pressure generated on the façade by the prevailing wind (bottom).

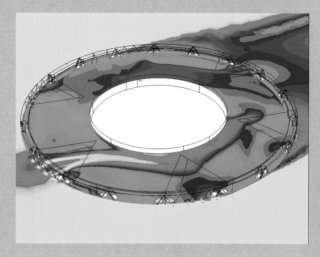

finish venetian blinds in the cavity back to the outside via an air-handling unit. The façade becomes part of the office-extract system. A solar transmission rate of 15% is obtained, greatly reducing reliance on mechanical ventilation and energy consumption while ensuring comfortable working conditions for the building's users. The conditioning plant is decentralized, floor by floor, using a six fan coil unit system, which allows the environment within the building to be fine-tuned to the needs of users and further reduces energy usage. The fresh-air supply and extractor units are contained within ceiling voids. Plant to power the system is located at basement level, with three-storey-high cooling towers located at level 35.

There are 792 triangular opening windows on the atria of levels 2–34. The windows serve two purposes: to provide natural ventilation and to extract smoke in case of a fire. The opening and closing of the windows is controlled by the building-management system, which receives information on external conditions from six weather stations located near the top of the building.

30 St Mary Axe

LONDON

The decision to install tinted glass in the spiralling atria, driven by practical considerations of glare and solar gain, gave the final building (opposite and above right) a distinctive appearance that inspired its official logo.

Pages 86–87
The cladding has not yet been installed on level four of the all-steel structure (10 February 2002).

Swiss Re was never prepared to agree to planting the atria." There were, as Walter Kielholz of Swiss Re explains, good reasons for what might have appeared a loss of nerve. "It could have been practical if we were occupying the whole building", he says. "But were tenants to be forced to live with the gardens?" In the case of the Commerzbank, the whole tower was occupied by one organization, and the gardens were enclosed spaces, whereas the diagram of 30 St Mary Axe provided for working office floors to be open to the voids. Sara Fox is forthright on the issue. "The practical problems were too great", she insists. "The maintenance burden was potentially huge. Anyway it became clear that the spaces were not going to support more than a small range of plants. They had to be shaded in some way, to combat glare, so the plants wouldn't get much light. We might have had to use artificial lighting, which seemed mad. And the opening windows would produce variable climatic conditions that were again not going to encourage plant growth." Fox set her mind firmly against sky gardens and the idea was clearly not going to fly. The image of a planted building seen in some of Foster's drawings was to remain no more than a vision. In the completed building the atria read, however, as distinctive diagonal bands across the façades. Since they are double-glazed spaces, some shading would always be a necessity.

The diagrid

The structural steel diagrid developed by Foster and Partners in association with Arup was fundamental to the realization of the radical form conceived for the building. The external diagrid responds to the curved shape of the tower, providing vertical support for the floors and allowing for the provision of column-free internal spaces. In effect, it represents a highly rational, efficient and economic strategy for the construction of a mould-breaking landmark building.

The diagrid is formed of simple straight circular sections of steel, connected by 360 steel nodes or junctions at the points where the geometry of the tower changes as the diameter of the floors first increases and then diminishes. The nodes, each of them about 2 metres high, consist of three steel plates welded together at varying angles to address the changing geometry of the structure, thus avoiding the need to fabricate individual end details to suit each location. The detailed design of the nodes was developed by steelwork contractor Victor Buyck-Hollandia. The success of the system depended on very exact fabrication: bearing surfaces were milled to a tolerance of 0.1 millimetres.

Assembled, the diagrid consists of a series of two-storey-high A-frames, placed end to end to form a frame that reads as a pattern of diamonds, since the cross bars are painted dark blue (that reads as black through the glazing) and the diagonals white. At every other floor, in line with the nodes, perimeter hoops encircle the building, counteracting the horizontal spread of the structure and binding the whole together, like the hoops on a barrel.

In addition to being highly efficient in resisting wind forces, the diagrid frames the atria, or lightwells, that spiral up the building. The atria are kept free of structure by inclining the perimeter columns to follow the helical path of the six-fingered floors up through the building. The diagrid can be read as a double spiral formed by the pattern of columns. Its structural efficiency is basic to the practical success of the building, since the core of the tower is not needed to resist wind forces and the amount of flexible floor space within it can be maximized.

Arup used computer modelling to resolve the complex geometry of the diagrid, as illustrated in light blue on the 3-D diagram.

The two-storey-high A-frames are assembled at plaza level and then hoisted into position by one of the three tower cranes. The central node (opposite, top) ingeniously solves the challenge of the varying geometries generated by the shape of the tower.

External glass louvres were considered but were ruled out as difficult to clean. Eventually it was decided to body-tint the glass.

Teamwork was key to the success of the 30 St Mary Axe project and it certainly drove Foster and Partners' contribution. With Robin Partington as director in charge, the team included Paul Scott, who was to see the project through to completion as project director in succession to Partington and whose role was to co-ordinate the consultants. Rob Harrison worked on the development of the tower design along with Simon Reed, who was tasked with the base of the building and the plaza. Paul Leadbeatter and Michael Gentz focused on the façade and cladding design with the help of Jacob Nørlov, who produced many of the early cladding models.

The distinctive form of the diagrid emerged even during the early stages of construction (20 February 2002).

STRUCTURE AND SERVICES

If the structure did not become a series of vertical gardens, it was to be a building that breathed and moved, an aerodynamic structure with an 'organic' twist. To achieve this vision Foster brought in a team of specialist engineers. A tall building of an earlier generation, for example the CU tower or Tower 42, was constructed around a massive central concrete core that formed its structural mainstay. The core of the CU tower measures 22.8 metres by 15 metres and supports a cantilevered steel frame, with concrete floors laid on it, from which the curtain-walled façades were hung. Internal columns were required to ensure the stability of the structure. In the case of 30 St Mary Axe, the façade is not simply a cladding but a key structural element. Architecture and structure were to be closely integrated.

Dominic Munro of Arup came to the project in 1999, when Foster's designs were fully developed and the push was on to submit a planning application. The ideas behind the building were clear, but how it was to be constructed remained to be decided. "The diagrid [external diagonal grid] had yet to emerge as a fundamental feature of the building", Munro says. The structural agenda of 30 St Mary Axe is far removed from that of the tall office buildings of the past, and it moved on from earlier Foster projects: the Japanese Millennium Tower had featured a diagrid, but structurally it was used as bracing for the vertical steel frame. 30 St Mary Axe is a steel-framed building. Steel construction came to dominate the London development scene during the 1980s, when American 'fast track' construction became the norm. The need then was for new financial sector buildings, delivered quickly. (Richard Rogers's Lloyd's Building took five years (1981–86) to construct; 30 St Mary Axe was built in thirty-three months.) Even the central core of the Swiss Re tower is constructed of steel, around 11,000 tonnes of which in total were used in the project. The steel structure had to respond to the radical form of the building, ensure stability, resist high winds and provide column-free office spaces inside, as well as facilitate the inclusion of the spiralling atria. To address the brief, the Arup team developed the diagrid system of intersecting steel sections that wrap the tower. It is the diagrid that supports the floors

An early working model showing the way the structure developed from a conventional vertical solution to a diagonal design.

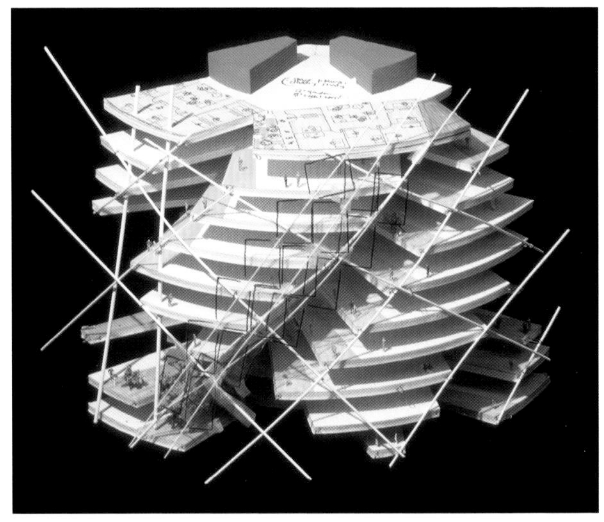

SKANSKA

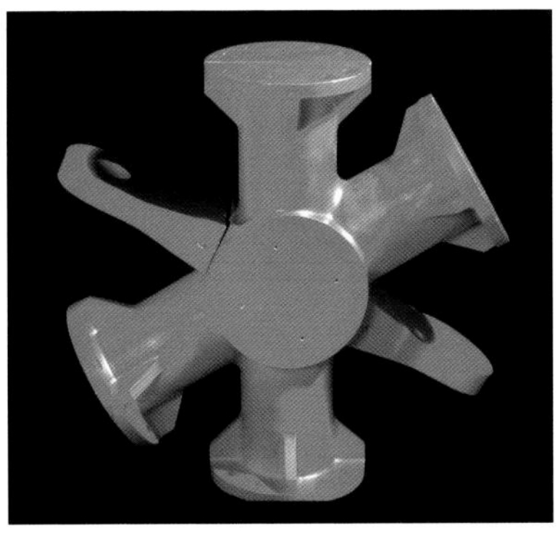

The structural nodes are an elegant engineering solution that unfortunately had to be encased in fire protection, creating a challenge for the design team to develop equally elegant cladding. An early design for a cast steel node (deemed impractical) is seen above.

and removes the need for columns in the office spaces. The diagrid consists of simple, straight circular steel sections, although these had to be enveloped in fire protection and encased in aluminium cladding. The columns get slimmer as they rise up the tower; Arup used computer modelling to design the steelwork in detail, so that the specialist steelwork contractor, Victor Buyck-Hollandia (VBH, a Dutch/Belgian joint venture operation), could fabricate the sections to the exact size required. "The structure depended on very accurate fabrication", Dominic Munro explains. "There was very little scope for mistakes. Fortunately VBH was absolutely outstanding; it was a major contributor to the success of the whole project."

The diagrid consists of a series of two-storey-high triangular A-frames, weighing up to 11 tonnes. Placed end to end, with the cross bars painted a very dark blue that reads as black through the glass and the diagonals white, the frame reads externally as a pattern of diamonds, each of which is four storeys high. The A-frames emerge to dramatic effect at the base of the tower. The fact that the tower bulges out, reaching its widest point at level 17, then narrows as it rises towards the crown, with floor sizes varying, means that the geometry of the frame is constantly changing. The steel columns forming the diagrid intersect at the point of the A-frames. There are 360 junctions or 'nodes', each up to 2 metres high and formed of three steel plates welded together at different angles in response to the differing floor diameters and tied back to the core by radial beams. (Paul Scott compares them to the spokes on a bicycle wheel.) These nodes, as the Arup team recognized from day one, were nothing less than the key to realizing the curvaceous form conceived by Foster. Their fabrication was an exacting task for the production

The radial steel beams tying the diagrid back to the core are likened to the spokes of a bicycle wheel (above left, 25 March 2002; left, 4 December 2001).

plants in The Netherlands and Belgium, where Arup's computer models were used by VBH to generate the vital components to very precise tolerances: the bearing surfaces of the nodes and columns were milled to a tolerance of 0.1 millimetres.

At every other floor, in line with the nodes and designed to counteract the horizontal forces generated by the shift in direction of the columns at that point, the building is held in by a hoop; these are similar, in principle, to the hoops around a wooden barrel. These were designed to take up an element of spread in the structure as the tower grew upwards. At its widest point around 50 millimetres could be added to the diameter of the tower, Dominic Munro explains. In March 2003 with the main structure of the building nearing completion, the *Sunday Times* carried an extraordinary report to the effect that the tower was "sagging" under the weight of its cladding, or even "sinking". The report was, of course, nonsense but it created, if briefly, another myth in the history of the project. As Arup pointed out, most buildings do sink slightly when constructed – around

Even-numbered floors are encircled by a 'hoop' of lateral steel beams that counter the natural outward spread as the load on the building increases (14 September 2002).

12 centimetres in the case of 30 St Mary Axe – but "in addition to the usual shortening movement present in all buildings, the unique shape of the perimeter steel diagrid structure causes a small outward spread of the lower levels during construction".

There is a neat – and far from coincidental – symmetry between the teamwork that characterized the 30 St Mary Axe project and the way in which it integrates architecture and engineering, structure and services, the practical and the visionary. For Foster and Partners, collaboration with engineers comes naturally; it is in this way that the practice has been a consistent innovator in structural and services issues. The regular brainstorming sessions held at Foster's office in Battersea, on the south bank of the Thames, attended often by Norman Foster and other directors as well as members of the Swiss Re team, structural and services engineers, contractors and other consultants, helped to thrash out problems as they arose. By working closely with the specialist contractors, the design team was able to do 'reality checks': "we had to reassure ourselves that what we had designed was achievable", says Michael Gentz of Foster and Partners. Everything about the project was unusual. The cladding contract would be highly demanding, it was clear, and the fully glazed, double-skin cladding (24,000 square metres in total) would have to be co-ordinated with the overall design of the casings for the structural steel. The Swiss specialist cladding manufacturer Schmidlin was awarded the contract in 2001 after an interview process and began working with the architects and engineers to refine the façade design. This was an area in which computers came into their own: new software was developed to cope with the complexities of the task.

Michael Gentz, a member of what Peter Holroyd of Swiss Re's project team calls the "technically brilliant group of people" who made up the Foster team, was heavily involved with the design of the façade after joining the team in 1998. The evolution of the column casing design involved building full-size mock-ups,

At one stage of the design process the team experimented with a cladding solution nicknamed the 'Zulu shield', which was mocked-up in Foster's offices (below left) and at full scale by specialist cladding manufacturer Schmidlin, in Switzerland (below).

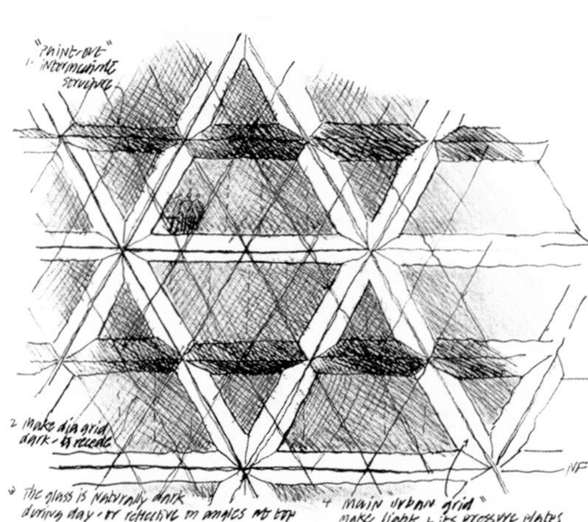

The cladding, initially developed in sketches by Norman Foster (above), was ultimately realized in detailed computer-generated drawings (right).

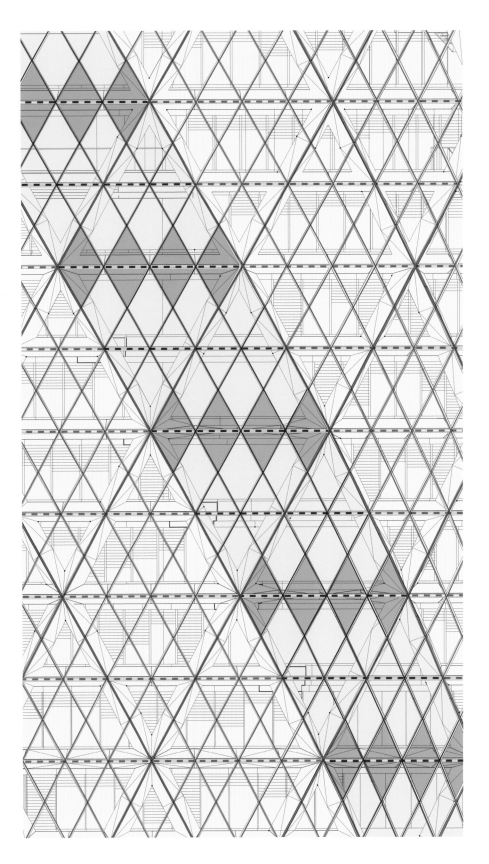

In order to test the visual impact of the cladding, as seen from the exterior through glass, a full-scale mock-up was constructed in Foster and Partners' offices in Battersea and viewed from the other side of the Thames, in both daytime and night-time conditions. It became clear that white was the only colour that read clearly through the glass and the 'Zulu shield' concept was abandoned.

experimenting with ideas of bending and folding aluminium. One issue was that the casings had to be large enough to allow for a degree of movement in the steel frame. There were proposals to reduce their apparent size by painting them in a 'Zulu shield' pattern, but this was eventually abandoned.

The façade of 30 St Mary Axe is much more than a simple skin enclosing internal space: it is a key element in the environmental design for the building. BDSP Partnership, which had worked on the Commerzbank Headquarters, was brought in by Foster at an early stage to work on this aspect of the tower. The curvilinear form of the building had already been established but was still to be refined. One obvious advantage of the circular plan was that the building would require up to 25% less external surface than a rectangular block of equivalent size, hence there was less scope for heat loss and solar gain. The tower would cost less and perform better. However, the benefits of the 'gherkin' form – the nick-name was being applied long before the building went on site – in terms of the environment around the building remained a matter of speculation. The Foster team's assumption was that the curvaceous tower would have a much more benign impact at ground level than its 1960s neighbour, the CU tower, which generates a notorious degree of turbulence at street level. BDSP's analysis confirmed this hypothesis and helped the architects to minimize the down-draught effect and make the plaza at the base of the tower a pleasant place to linger. It was calculated that the curvilinear shape produced around 40% of the down-draught of a square building of equivalent size. The BDSP team, under Sinisa Stankovic, also helped develop the idea of using natural ventilation as part of a mixed-mode cooling system in which the option of using air conditioning was also provided. Natural ventilation offered the user a supply of fresh air free of charge,

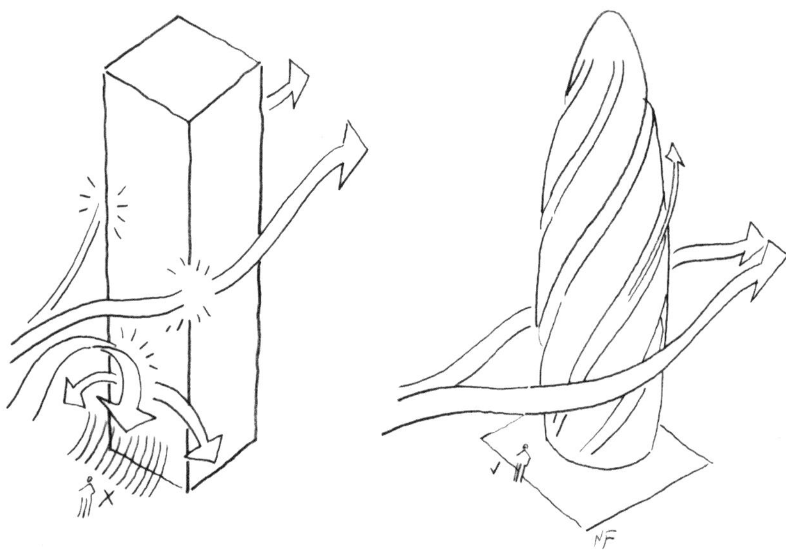

Whereas conventional orthogonal or square towers generate turbulence at ground level, the impact of a circular building is significantly less.

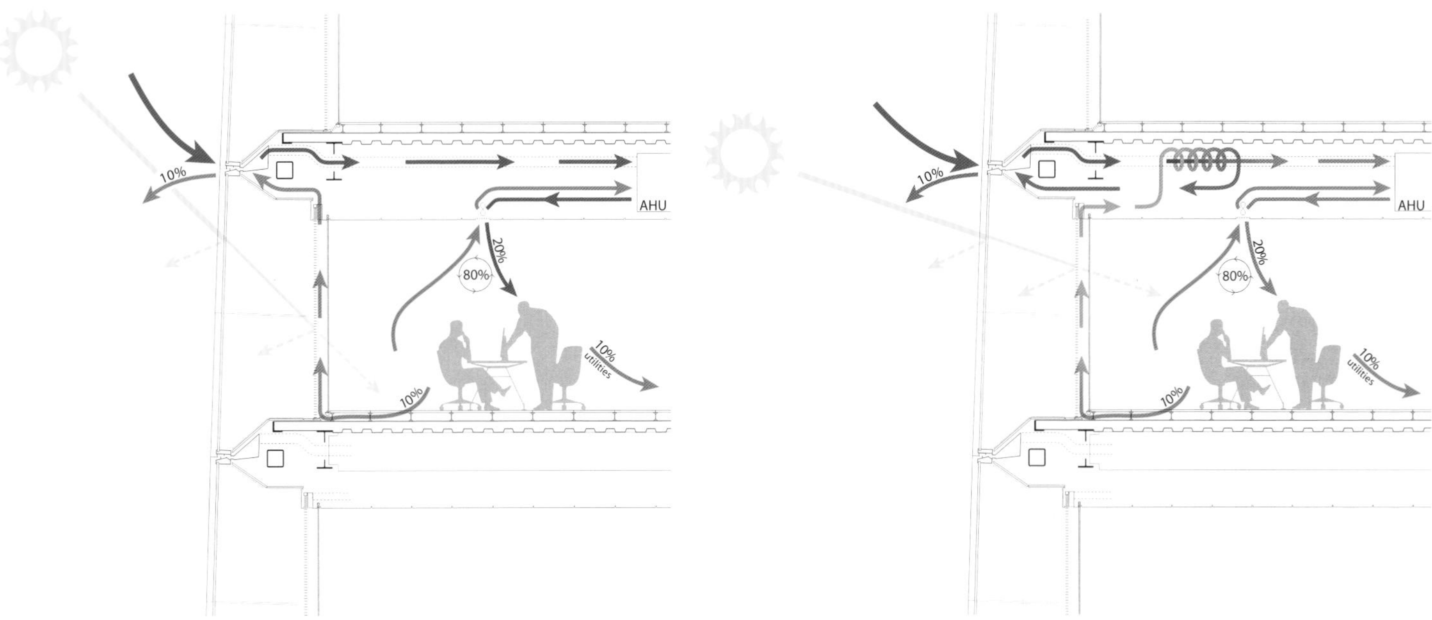

The sections above illustrate the ventilation strategy in the summer (above) and winter (above right).

Wind tunnel tests confirmed the benefits of the circular form and inspired the team to consider natural ventilation options.

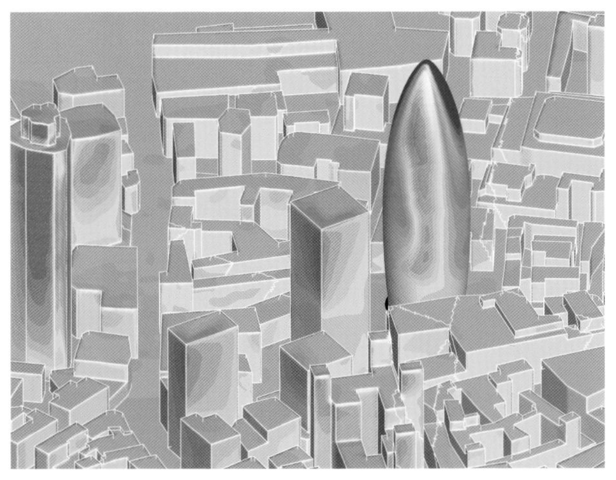

but the problem with tall buildings is that draughts can cause havoc if windows have to be left open. The installation of a computerized building management system would allow for external conditions to be monitored. By installing the opening windows in the atria, fresh air could be channelled across the office floors via the buffer zone of the atria, with the air pressure differential on the exterior of the building driving the ventilation. Finally, the façade played a role in insulating the building and baffling solar gain. The double skin, with a cavity of around 1.2 metres on average between external cladding and the internal layer of glazing, would be fitted with Venetian blinds to cut out the glare of the sun and reduce solar gain. In summer cool fresh air from the offices would be vented at floor level into the cavity, cooling glass and blinds, before being extracted at ceiling level through fan-assisted ducts. The combination of these elements results in a reduction of solar gain of 85%. In winter warm air from offices would have the opposite effect, cancelling out the customary chilling effect of a glass façade.

Matthew Kitson, who had worked for BDSP, subsequently joined Hilson Moran Partnership and, with director Jim Hilson, worked with Foster to establish the precise form of the tower, using computational fluid dynamics, a technology also used to design racing cars and, in effect, a type of computerized wind tunnel test. As consultants for the mechanical and electrical engineering of 30 St Mary Axe, Hilson Moran turned the initial environmental strategy into a fully designed services programme. Any large office building requires extensive areas of plant, *i.e.* water tanks, sprinkler tanks, heating boilers, electrical distribution equipment,

It is not generally recognized that a second six-storey building was erected next to the tower. 20 Bury Street, located on the north-east corner of the site, houses the boilers for the tower in its top two floors, thus eliminating the need for unsightly flues near the top of the main building.

Overleaf
By removing the services from the top of the tower, a spectacular social space is created with stunning 360-degree views across London.

coolers and chillers, as well as air conditioning equipment. In a typical office building of the last few decades, these will generally occupy the upper levels. One of the innovative moves of the so-called High-tech school of design was to detach service areas from workspace areas. The idea of 'served' and 'servant' spaces drove the design of Rogers's Lloyd's Building, with its distinctive service towers, and was reflected in Norman Foster's Hongkong and Shanghai Bank. Both buildings were completed in 1986. By the end of the twentieth century, however, with the increasing awareness of the environmental damage caused by modern buildings, the emphasis had shifted from issues of the location of plant towards the reduction of its bulk and of dependence on mechanical services.

It would have been an obvious step to use the top of the tower as a location for services, as the floors in this part are too small to be useful as offices. For Richard Griffiths, this seemed a highly practical approach that made good use of the space. Norman Foster was, however, determined to retain the top of the tower as a social space, preferably a public one but at the very least an area accessible to all the building's users. For Robin Partington, it had the potential to become "the most spectacular room in Europe" and was an obvious location for a restaurant and hospitality suite. As Paul Scott recalls, "Swiss Re had to be convinced that this was a good strategy; there had to be a business case as well as an architectural one. When that case was clearly put, they accepted it." Today the idea of 30 St Mary Axe without its remarkable top of the building space seems inconceivable, but Walter Kielholz is pragmatic about the issue. "It's a good investment, like the entire building", he says. "It's booked for evening events by City organizations all year round – all very good for the image of the company."

In the completed building, heavy plant such as tanks, chillers and electrical distribution equipment is located in the basement. The four gas boilers powering the heating are placed in the top floors of the separate six-storey building on Bury Street. Up at level 35 six closed circuit cooling towers, which are three storeys tall and are connected to basement chillers, were chosen for their efficiency and reduced consumption of water and chemicals. (Measures were taken to minimize visible exhaust flues from the towers: "we didn't want the tower looking like a Saturn 5 rocket set for take off", says Kitson.) Fundamental to the services programme was the decision to decentralize the air conditioning plant floor by floor. This was done partly for architectural reasons – to remove the need for intermediate plant floors with louvres – but equally for environmental ones. The aspiration of the services programme is to ensure that only those services required locally are in operation; this is the antithesis of the overall air conditioning found in most North American office buildings and also adopted at Canary Wharf. The programme facilitates the balanced use of air conditioning and natural ventilation in line with the preferences of individual users. Various systems were considered to power the air conditioning, including chilled beams or ceilings, which proved

impractical. Fan coil units, which introduce and extract air floor by floor, were specified, combining efficiency with economy. Heat recovery units are installed to maximize the effectiveness of the air conditioning. For Robin Partington, the chosen strategy is most significant for its flexibility: "the energy consumption of the building can be controlled floor by floor, finger by finger. It isn't radical in the sense of reinventing the wheel, but by London standards it is highly progressive."

Hilson Moran used computerized environmental modelling throughout the period of development for the project to establish the performance of the building. Every aspect of the tower, from the lobby to the top of building hospitality area, was subjected to close analysis and the findings fed into the building management system. The design of the façade was a critical issue in securing the target of using much less energy than that used by a traditionally serviced office building of similar size. The energy saving relies on 30 St Mary Axe operating in mixed-mode configuration (with the windows open) for up to 40% of the year. The final façade design – it is an "active ventilated façade" – developed the ideas contained in the initial studies. Hilson Moran appraised fourteen options for the façade in the light of cost, performance and maintenance criteria. Air extracted from the offices is passed through the cavity and air handling units also extract heat reflected by the blinds.

For some critics there is something perverse about designing an all-glass building and then devising ways of combating solar gain. Yet Norman Foster is unrepentant. The high building is, for him, a chance for humanity to use technology to good effect and benefit from views and the sense of liberation from the city streets; from the earliest times, men have sought to build high. Foster points out that people in the building have views not only directly out of the windows, but also across the office floors and down to the street; from some points much of central London can be glimpsed. 30 St Mary Axe was seen, in some quarters, as extreme when first planned, a break with the North American direction that London office buildings had taken with the boom of the 1980s. Yet, as Matthew Kitson points out, new EU legislation, the incoming Part L of the Building Regulations and the sustainable design provisions contained in the Mayor of London's draft supplementary planning guidance document published in spring 2005 could spell the end of high-energy buildings in London. Where 30 St Mary Axe, and Swiss Re, led, the rest of the world of development looks set to follow.

St Paul's Cathedral is visible to the west (above) and Canary Wharf to the east (opposite).

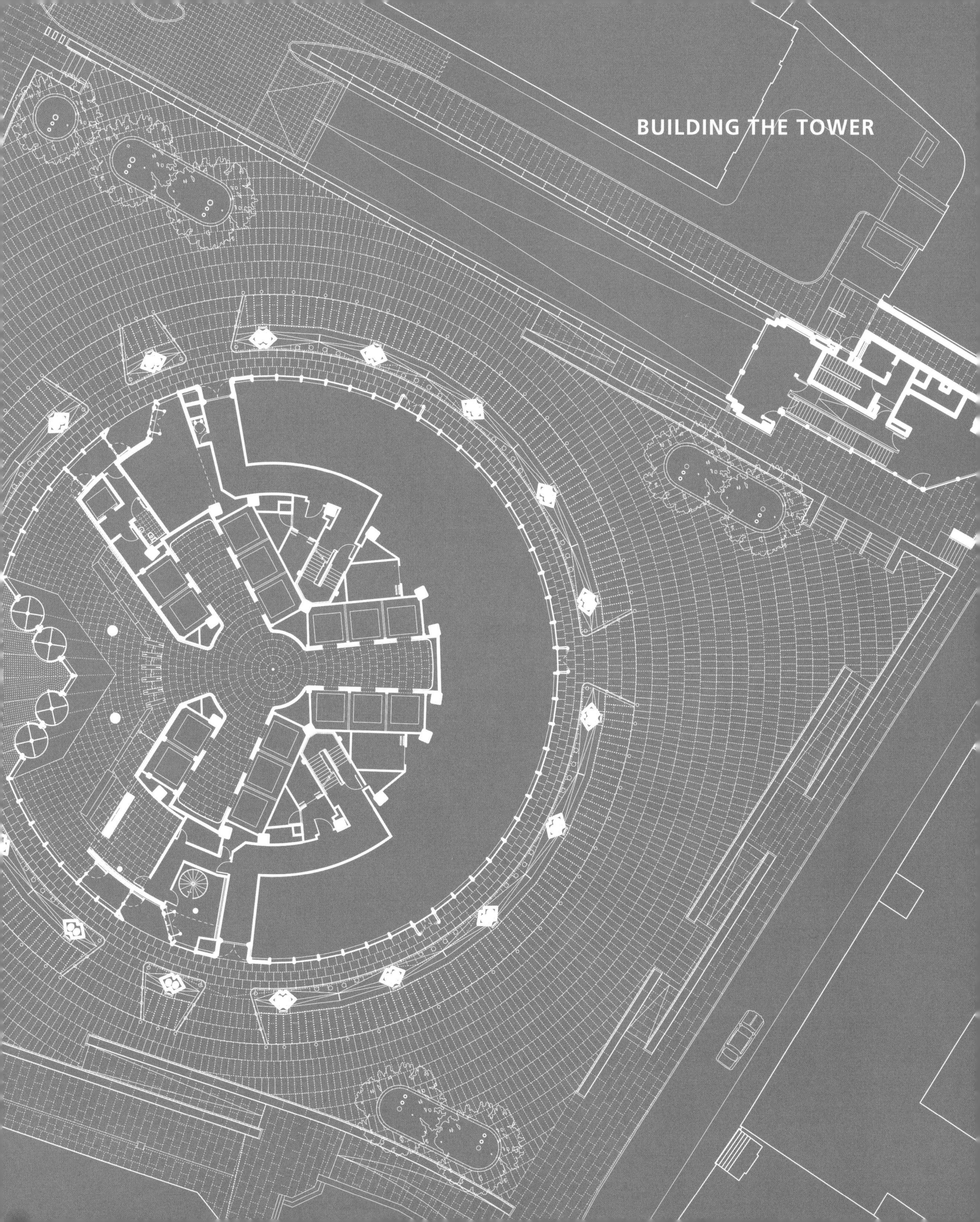

BUILDING THE TOWER

SKANSKA

SKANSKA
SKANSKA

SAMSUNG
020 7643 10,00
keltbray

BUILDING THE TOWER

BASE BUILDING CONSTRUCTION

Swiss Re finally concluded its purchase of the St Mary Axe site in January 2001. Skanska, the vendor, had acquired Kvaerner's construction business and with it the agreement with Swiss Re to carry out the construction project. Work started on site immediately, the demolition of the Baltic Exchange remains having begun before Christmas, with every reusable element on the site carefully retained for recycling, including London stock bricks, parquet flooring and steelwork. The aim was to complete the shell and core project by September 2003. Swiss Re had proved a predictably tough client, negotiating a reduction of four months from Skanska's preferred schedule.

Opposite
9 February 2001: The remains of the old Baltic Exchange are cleared during demolition, a process that extended over three months.

15 February 2001: The carved pediment from the Bury Street façade of the old Baltic Exchange is salvaged during demolition.

Piling

30 St Mary Axe sits on 333 piles drilled to approximately 25 metres into the ground. The piles extend down through the river terrace gravels and 'made ground' (layers of historical foundations and soil deposits), with the majority of the pile length drilled into the London clay beneath, the top of which lies approximately 10 metres below street level. The pattern of the piles reflects the structure they underpin, with a ring supporting the diagrid and a grouping of piles forming a circle supporting the main core of the tower.

Drilling the shafts and then filling them with concrete (as opposed to driving pre-cast concrete piles or steel sections) reduced the noise levels of this work, a key factor with planners given the location of the site in the heart of the City. Three piling rigs were used to bore shafts down into the clay. The piles are 750 millimetres in diameter where they sit in the clay, while their upper sections were drilled slightly wider to allow a steel casing to be temporarily inserted to the depth of the overlying gravels and made ground. The steel casing is necessary because these soils allow the ground water to flow and would cause the drilled shaft to collapse if not 'sealed off'. Within the clay, water does not flow and thus the drilling could proceed without the casing. In addition, care was taken not to drill too deep, as further sand layers exist below the clay – those holding the main London aquifer (subterranean water reservoir) – which could also cause the shafts to collapse if encountered.

Once the shafts had been drilled to the required depth, reinforcing cages, 10–12 metres long, made off-site, were dropped into the holes and concrete was poured in. Each shaft required approximately two to three lorry loads of concrete. The steel casings were removed for reuse directly after the concreting, prior to the concrete setting within a few hours of being placed.

On a very tight site, surrounded by roads and neighbouring buildings, there was a limit to the speed at which piling could be done. The piling operations therefore had to be carefully co-ordinated to ensure that the removal of spoil did not get in the way of the delivery of equipment and materials to site, or cause unnecessary traffic congestion. The creation of a piling 'mat', formed from compacted fill, further facilitated these operations.

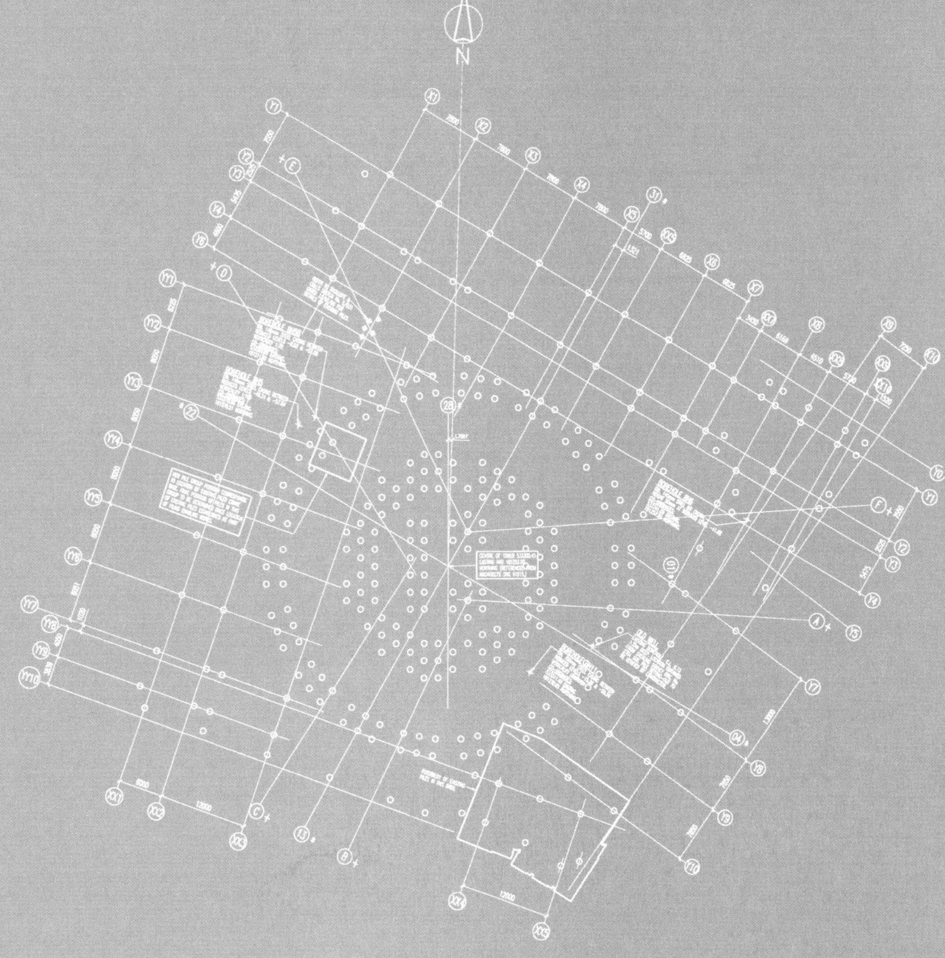

Right
In the piling diagram, the outer double ring of piles reflects the external diagrid structure, while the central core is supported by its own formation of piles.

Below, left to right
End of March to July 2001: The piles are drilled, extending down to approximately 25 metres; the reinforcing cages are delivered to the site, ready to be inserted into the pile hole; the concrete is then poured into the pile hole; the casing is removed, before the concrete is fully set, to be reused for the next pile; a section of completed piles.

9 July 2001: The reinforcing cage, 30 metres in diameter, 2.6 metres deep and weighing approximately 156 tonnes, nears completion, prior to the pouring of the concrete to form the central pile cap. There are a further 86 tonnes of reinforcement in the outer ring pile cap for the diagrid.

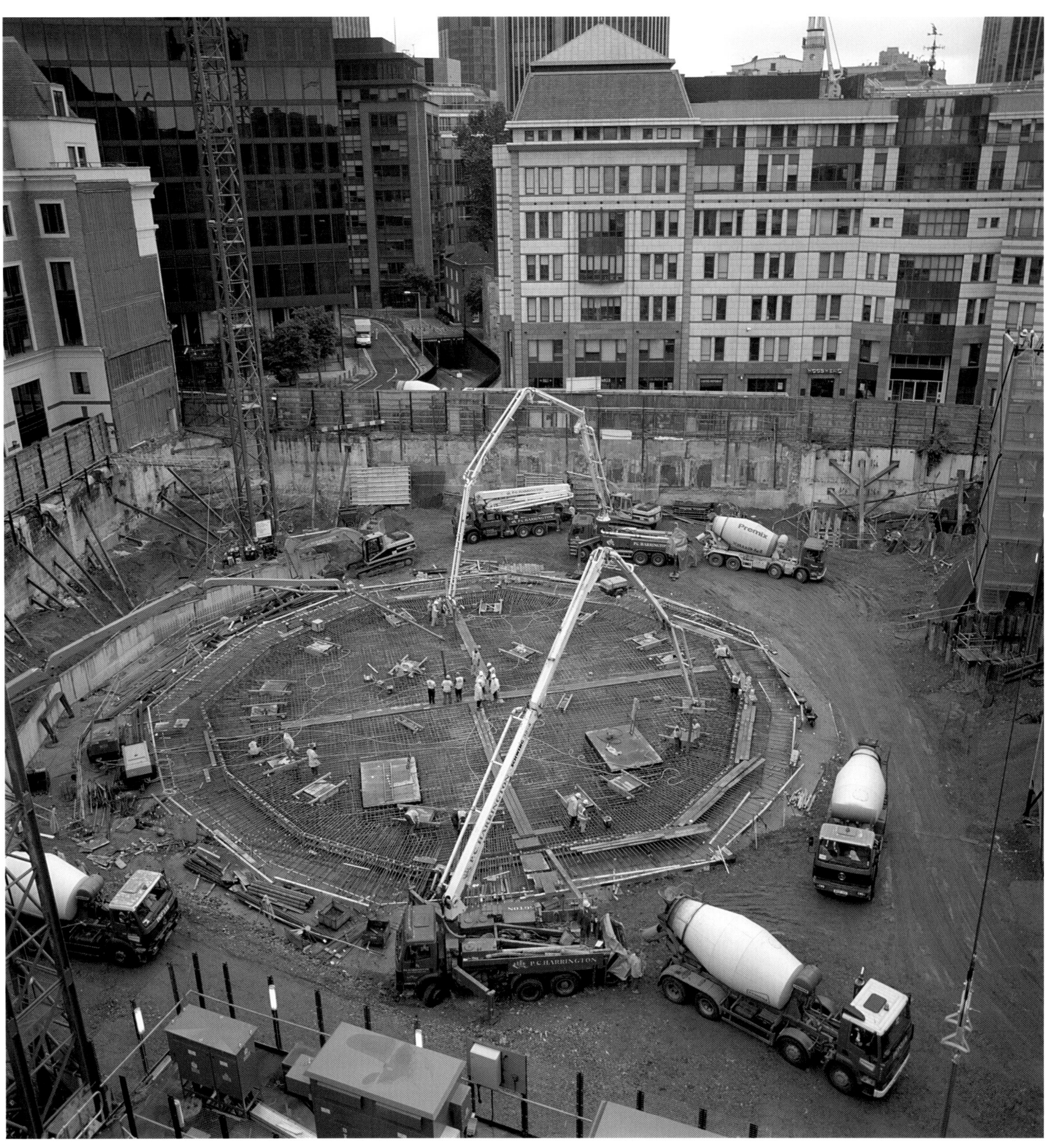
Premix
P.C.HARRINGTON

With the site cleared, work could start on the foundations for the tower, 333 permanent ones and 40 temporary, each 750 millimetres in diameter and up to 30 metres deep. The main problem that the contractors faced was the confined nature of the City site, which is surrounded by roads and buildings, and provided no space for the storage of materials. When it came to casting the main pile cap on which the tower would sit, almost 1800 cubic metres of concrete had to be poured in one continuous operation, with 290 vehicle movements in and out of the site over an eleven-hour period. Because of the number of truckloads of concrete, it was essential to schedule the work on a weekend when impact on traffic would be minimized.

14 July 2001: The main concrete pile cap that supports the whole of the building is poured in a massive operation lasting an entire day.

12 October 2001: The start of steel ceremony was hosted by Peter Forstmoser, Chairman of Swiss Re, and Mark Field, MP for the Cities of London and Westminster, along with a gathering including representatives of the project team and City Corporation. The first A-frame was signed by the VIP guests who attended, among them Norman Foster.

Shortly after the news of the '9/11' terrorist attacks in the USA broke, work began on the central core of the tower, a steel-framed structure. Its construction proceeded four to six floors ahead of the external diagrid; the superstructure was used to support three external climbing cranes that could be used to hoist the massive steel elements into position. The start of steel in October 2001 saw the first A-frame ceremonially installed. Steel, supplied by Victor Buyck-Hollandia, rose at an average rate of a floor a week when weather conditions permitted; cranes could not be used to hoist steel when wind speeds exceeded 34 miles per hour. As the diagrid rose up the tower, two storeys at a time, the decking followed a couple of floors behind.

By October 2001 the central core is visible, rising four to six storeys or more above the diagrid, which is then tied back to the core with radial steel beams upon which is laid the steel decking (below left, 25 October 2001; below right, 26 November 2001; opposite, 23 August 2002).

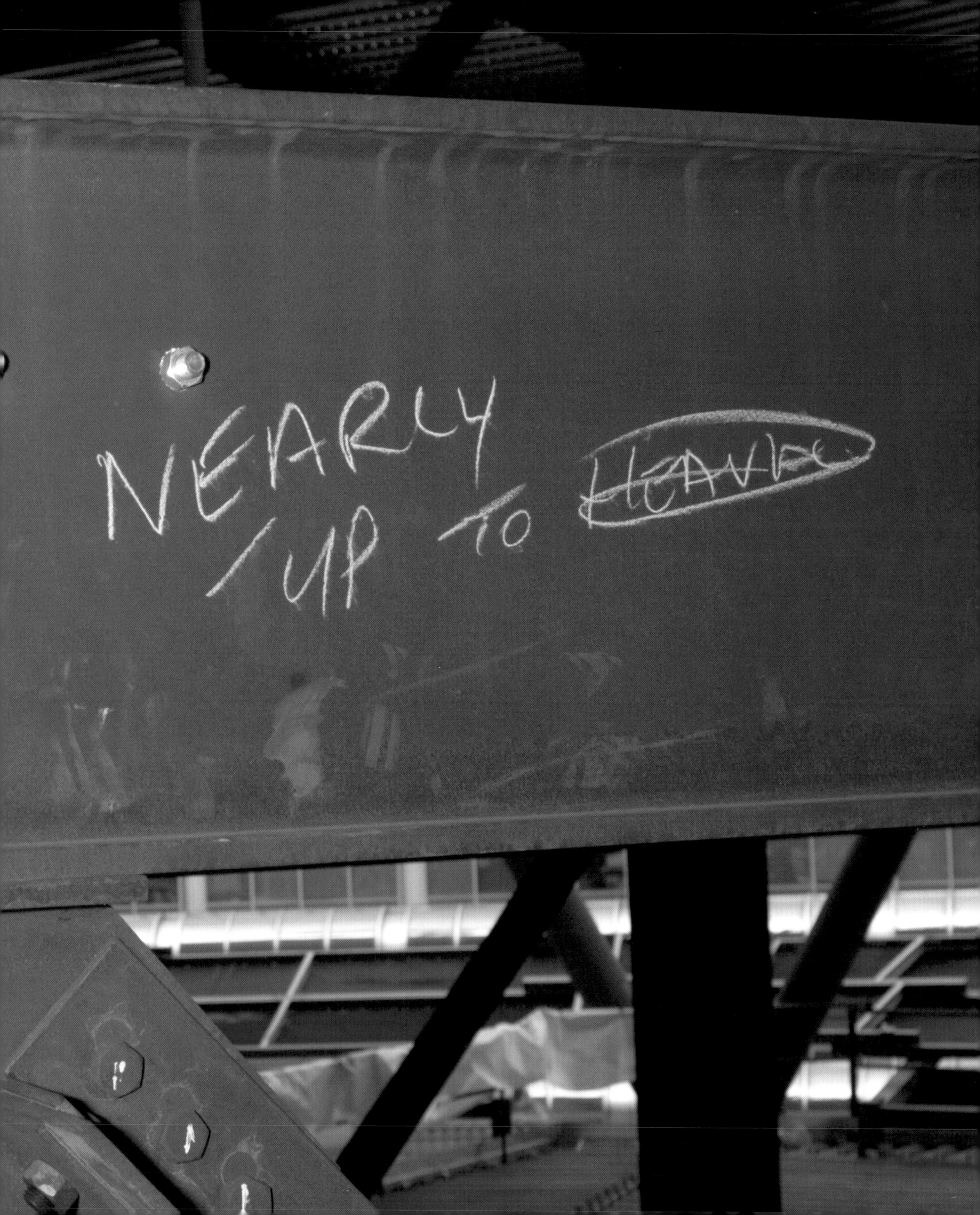
NEARLY
UP TO

25 March 2002: At the 15th level, the A-frames are tied to each other by steel beams and back to the core, ready to receive steel decking to form the floor.

11 January 2002 (opposite) to 7 October 2002 (right): As the steel structure of the building rises, the diameter of the A-frame columns reduces, reflecting the diminishing structural loads. The A-frame on the left is being installed on the sixth floor and has a diameter of 508 mm, while the A-frame on the right, only 273 mm in diameter, is destined for the 36th and 37th floors, where the plant rooms are located. The A-frames at the plant levels are exposed to the elements, and are therefore coated to prevent corrosion.

Opposite
4 April 2002: The structural steel ribbed decking on floor seven is fixed in place prior to the installation of the reinforcing bars and mesh.

8 March 2002: Concrete, which has been pumped from plaza level at high pressure, is spread to form the finished floor slab (with a depth of 160 mm) on floor four.

The single most expensive element in the construction budget was the cladding contract. Cladding manufacturer Schmidlin's team followed no faster than four to six floors behind the concreted slabs, installing the diamond-shaped curtain wall components. These were pre-assembled in Switzerland and designed to interlock on site. The cladding had to be installed in a precise position while still allowing for the movement inherent in the steel structure. The issue of differing tolerances was addressed by a specially designed bracket interface between cladding and steel. A scaffold tower supporting hoists on the exterior of the building was used to deliver men and materials to all levels. From the start the site had attracted huge public interest. The viewing windows cut into the surrounding hoardings were used by City workers to monitor the progress of the much-discussed project. From the immediate vicinity, in fact, it was impossible to see the top of the tower, and a rumour spread that technical problems had halted work on the upper storeys; views from a more distant vantage point revealed that this was far from the case.

Above
17 October 2002: On floor 21 Schmidlin's team installs the panels of tinted glass in the atrium.

Opposite
4 November 2002: The view from St Paul's Cathedral shows the progress of the cladding rising up the tower.

Overleaf
A detailed view of cladding panels shows their interlocking profiles.

Cladding

Top to bottom
A specially designed machine, nicknamed Robota, has six pneumatically operated suction pads that allow it to pick up and position the cladding panels, each weighing approximately 750 kilograms. The panels were delivered to the floor above their final destination and had to be manoeuvred from inside the building to the exterior, where they were attached to a remotely controlled crane unit.

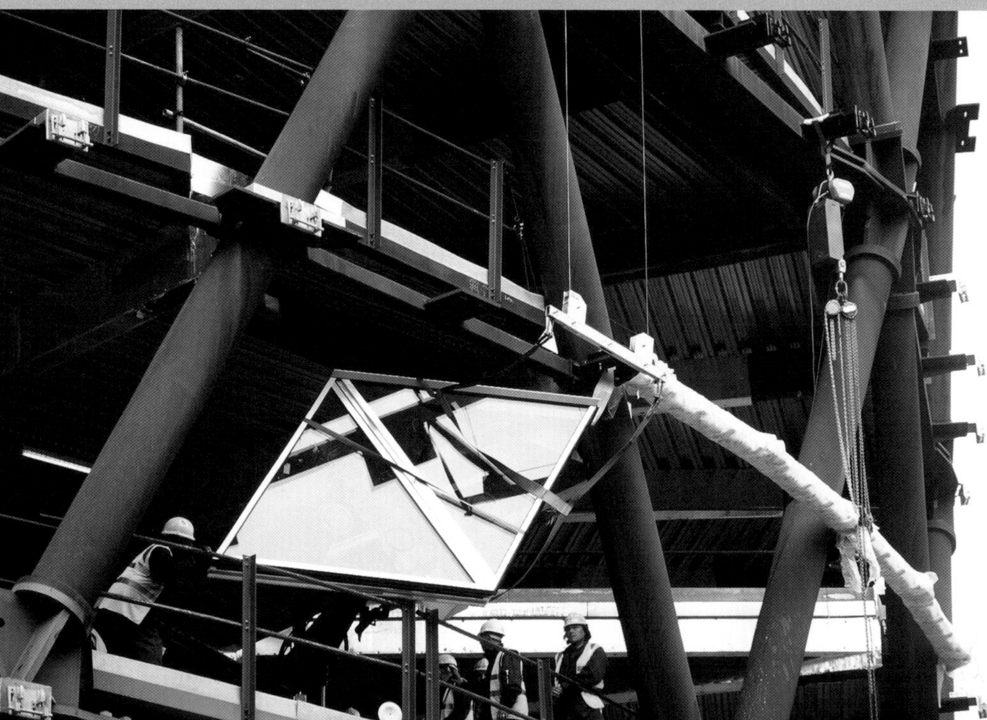

Left and below
Once the cladding unit has been orientated properly Robota's suction pads are released, allowing the mobile crane unit to take the full weight of the panel and to lower it into its final position.

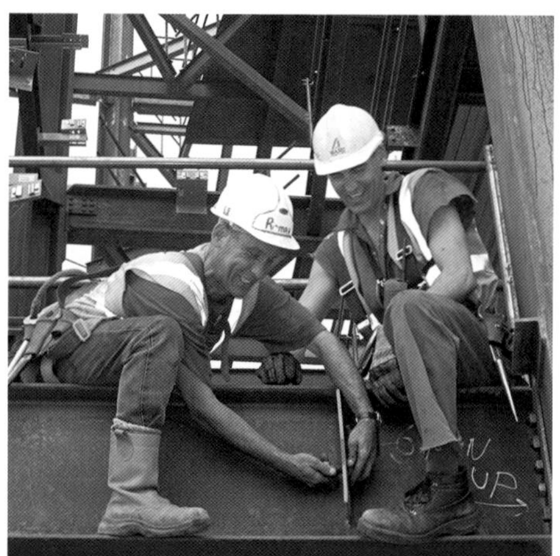

During the course of the project, more than 6000 construction workers were involved in the building.

16 August 2002: The triangular atria, spiralling at five degrees per floor, are marked externally by the tinted glazing, which provides both glare and thermal protection to the atria.

17 October 2002: A view from the interior of a six-storey atrium looks down from the 20th floor to the base at level 16. The steel structure is yet to be encased in fire protection and the powder-coated aluminium cladding.

3 May 2002: The staircases, formed of pre-assembled flights, are steadily installed as the tower steelwork progresses, with a crane threading the units down through the steel frame of the core.

Right
11 July 2002: The early installation of the staircases allowed for more efficient movement of men and materials throughout the building.

25 September 2002: The 'manbox', seen here from the 25th floor, attached to the crane hook, was the only means of transporting the steel erectors to the very top of the structure.

Left to right
The progress of the tower, seen from Tower 42 looking east toward Canary Wharf; 24 April 2002; 16 August 2002; 22 January 2003; 19 March 2003. The scaffolding structure to the left of the tower provided support for the external hoists, which ultimately rose to the 30th floor. The masts of the three tower cranes increased in height with the building.

Overleaf
23 January 2003: View from the south with Richard Rogers's Lloyd's Building in the foreground. The final form of the tower emerges, with the internal white diagrid casing clearly visible up to mid-point and the cooling towers sitting on level 35. The assembly of the steel-domed section has begun.

Left to right
The 'long ladder' sections delivered from Waagner-Biro's factory in Austria are assembled together at plaza level and hoisted up to the dome. Once in their final position, they are welded together.

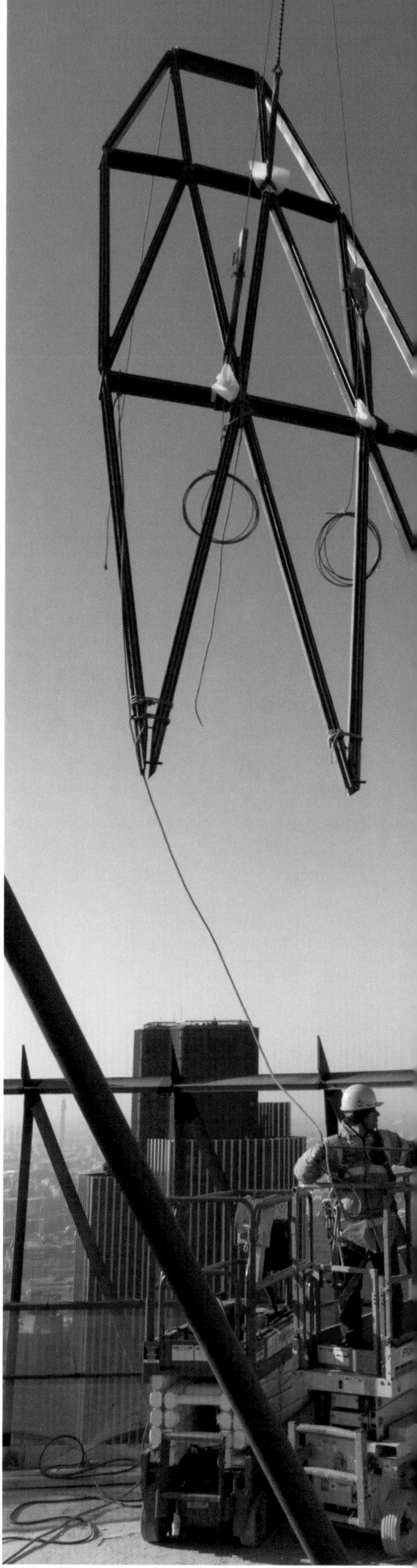

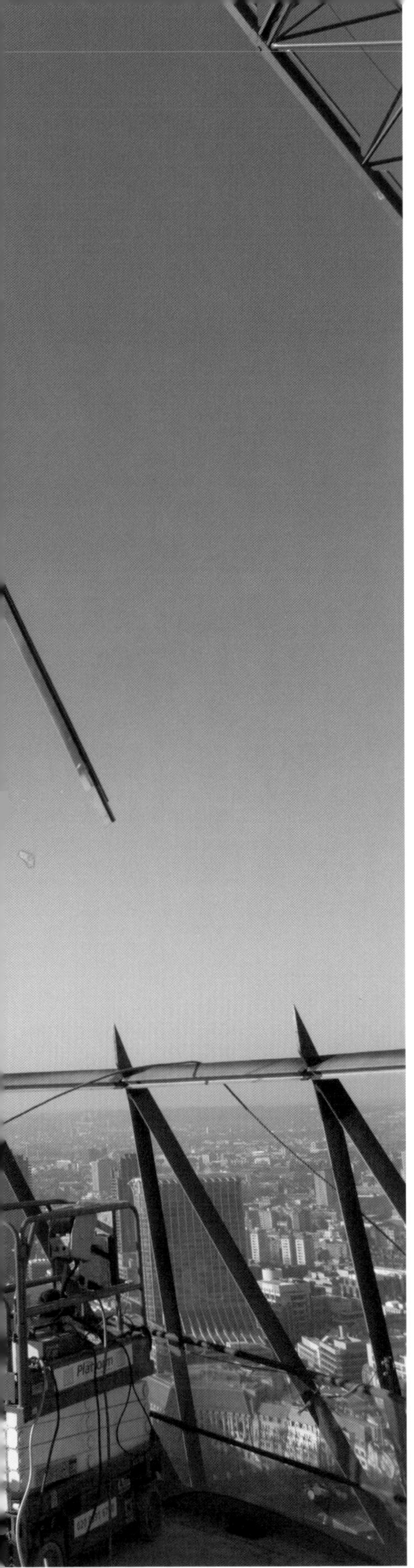
Platform

21 February 2003: At the centre of the dome a temporary cylindrical structure provides support for the dome framework until such time as it is complete and fully self-supporting.

The construction of the top three floors of the building, level 38 containing private dining-rooms, level 39 a restaurant and level 40 a bar, attracted a lot of attention. The very specialized nature of the job – this would be an all-steel structure, whereas the rest of the cladding was of aluminium, concealing the structural steel – demanded an expert team. A glazing system that could be attached directly to the steel framework by means of pressure plates was devised by Waagner-Biro, a specialist Austrian steelwork company that also worked on Norman Foster's spectacular Great Court roof at the British Museum. The dome at 30 St Mary Axe is 22 metres tall. It consists of eight horizontal hoops, diminishing in diameter as the building tapers and infilled with a trellis of glazed triangular panels, and reads as a continuous skin with the cladding of the lower floors. The steelwork was lifted up by crane after being partially prefabricated in Austria, with segments assembled at ground level and the final structure welded together at the top. The glazing (a glass 'sandwich', body-tinted and coated to combat solar gain) was installed by a team of abseilers, or, more accurately, access technicians, using the site tower cranes to deliver the panels. They were highly trained climbers,

19 March 2003: Finally, the pre-assembled top section of the dome, affectionately termed the 'spider', is hoisted into place. The three red lights on the outside of the framework are the high-level aircraft warning lights.

Overleaf
19 March 2003: The 'spider' is lowered into place. It will eventually hold at its centre the only curved piece of glass in the building.

32
ED10

X32E
D46

Top of the building

At the top of the tower, three floors (levels 38–40) are contained within a steel-framed dome that sits on top of the structural diagrid. The dome is the spectacular crown of the building and contains not services – the usual fate of top floors in tall buildings of an earlier generation – but striking social spaces, including a restaurant, a bar and a series of private dining-rooms.

These floors are the smallest in the tower and impractical as office spaces: the uses they accommodate capitalize on the building's magnificent panoramic views across much of London. However, the need to incorporate a range of facilities – including lifts, escape/fire stairs, WCs, kitchens, service risers and plant rooms – posed an enormous challenge for the architects. The resulting design of these spaces is a masterpiece of compression, providing five private dining-rooms, a restaurant with around sixty covers, and a spacious bar.

On the 39th and 40th floors, it is the awesome height of the space internally, and the impression of being surrounded by sky, that makes the 'top of the building' one of the great interiors of London.

To access these floors, it is necessary to change from the main lift system at level 34 to special geared-traction shuttle lifts, which take you to level 39. The bar area 'floats' above the restaurant, and presented a further challenge in the need to provide full disabled access. A glass-enclosed lift was considered, but would have intruded into the 40th-floor bar space, which is limited in size, and have eliminated the 360-degree view that can be seen today. Instead, a hydraulic hoist, a circular platform powered from below and which requires no 'box', was installed, rising up the centre of the circular staircase that connects these floors.

Top to bottom
Plans of floors 40, 39 and 38.

April 2003: Unlike the Schmidlin cladding on the lower parts of the building, the glazing on the dome was moved into position from the outside, using a similar suction pad system but requiring abseilers to guide the panels manually into position and mechanically fix it from the exterior.

Overleaf
20 May 2003: Glass installation progresses on the dome, using the same tinted glass as that on the atria below.

working outside the building using ropes and tackle in wind speeds of up to 30 miles per hour. When the wind speed was greater, work had to be suspended. Waagner-Biro planned to install up to fifteen glazed panels a day; on some days as many as twenty-seven were fitted. The final component in the dome was a single piece of glass made in Finland, a curved lens 2.42 metres across, the only piece of curved glass in the building and the crowning element of the tower. During its installation the Waagner-Biro team somehow tightened a bolt too much and the glass cracked; Sara Fox winces still at the memory. The symbolic act of completion had to await the delivery of a fresh piece of glass.

Above and overleaf
20 June 2003: Once the glass is installed in the dome, abseilers continue to work outside to complete the weather-proofing seals and final architectural elements.

Fox recalls that there had been worries about the success of the top of the building spaces. How would they be kept cool? The Foster team had been to see the roof-top 'glass bubble' boardroom at the Lingotto, the former Fiat factory in Turin, Italy, converted by Renzo Piano into a conference and cultural centre. "They had to retrofit elements to deal with heat and acoustics problems", Fox says. Natural ventilation was not possible at this level of the building because of high wind levels and the proximity of extractors from restaurants and toilets. Hilson Moran's solution, as energy-conscious as was practicable for this part of the building, was to air-condition the occupied space only, using a displacement air system

20 June 2003: The 'lens', 2.42 metres across, is positioned at the centre of the 'spider'.

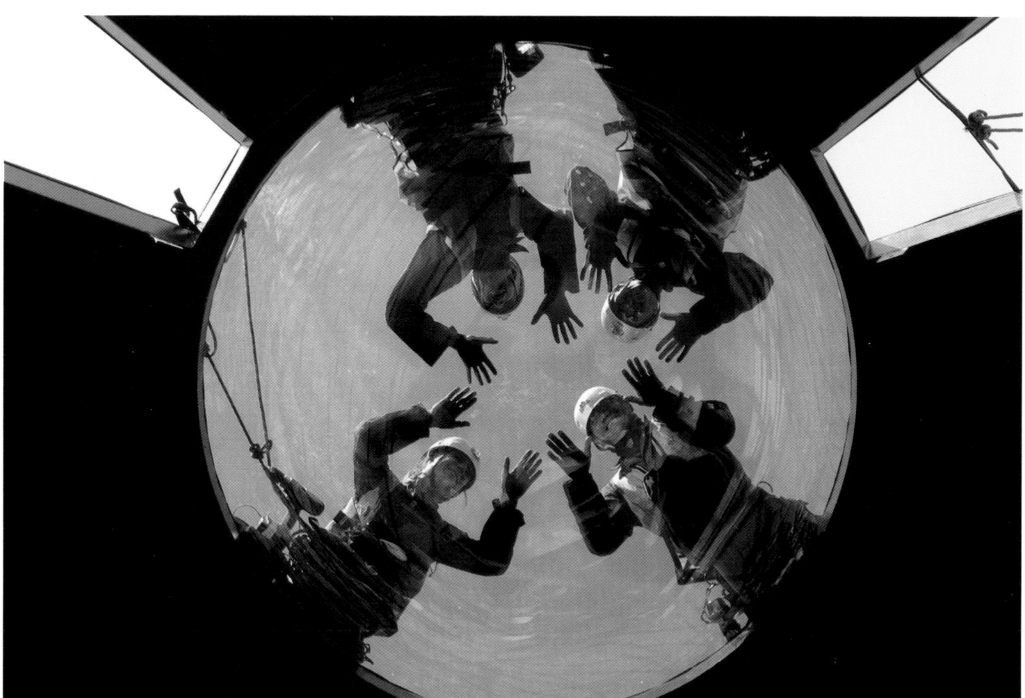

Below
The idea of a giant solar shade, which was to have been installed on the interior of the dome, was ultimately rejected as unnecessary.

Right
Every detail of the restaurant was carefully thought out to ensure that it complemented the space, including changing the colour of the table linens from white in the day to dark blue at night-time to reduce reflection on the glass.

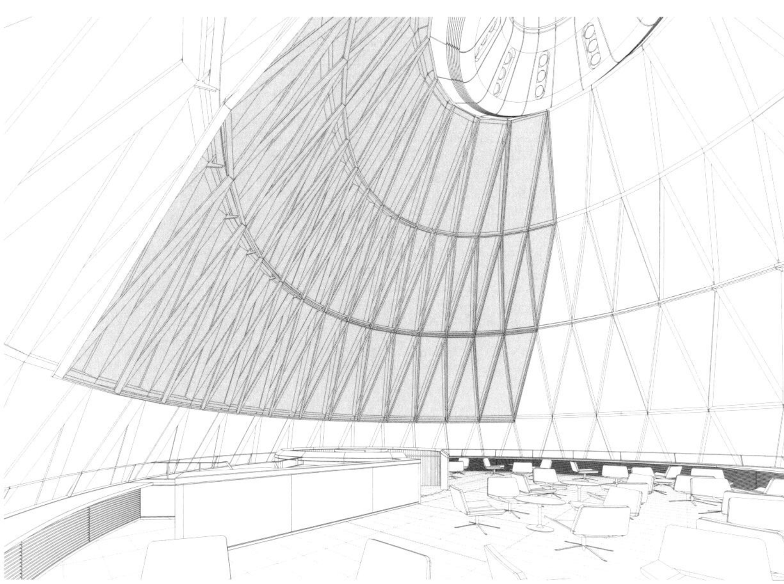

with chilled floors and high-level extract fans. Additionally, a rotating, solar-tracking shading device was designed to fit inside the dome at the summit to baffle direct sunlight, but was never installed as it proved to be unnecessary. Every detail has been considered to realize the full potential of this 'window on the world', even down to replacing white table linens with dark blue ones for use in the restaurant at night, so avoiding distracting reflections on the glass.

A glass tower needs to be kept clean. Abseiling was not a viable option when it came to the external cleaning of the glass that was required periodically. The Foster team was challenged to design a safe and practical cleaning system. On level 36 of the tower there is a 'garage' from which a two-person cleaning cradle can be lowered using a hoist that runs on rails within the building. The rails on which the cradle moves form a prominent, but necessary, feature of the exterior. Below the central 'bulge' of the building (from level 17 downwards) the cradle has to be restrained by a series of pins, although the bottom two floors can be cleaned from the plaza. For the top floors a five-stage extendable boom is supplied with room for two operatives. At its maximum length it extends to 30 metres, and reaches the lens at the very top of the building.

Left
Two conventional window-cleaning cradles are used to clean the exterior of the building below level 36. The cradles hang from booms that extend outwards as the cradle lowers and the building widens.

Opposite
Above level 36 a 'cherry picker' allows access all the way to the lens at the very top.

Window cleaning

30 St Mary Axe is externally fully glazed: internally its occupants enjoy natural light and exceptional views, but externally the glass needs to be kept clean. A typical tall building is cleaned using cradles suspended from the flat top that simply move up and down the façades.

Foster's design did not, however, lend itself to this treatment, ruling out the usual procedures. The top of the building is a tapering glazed pavilion containing a restaurant and bar, while below level 17 the circumference of the tower gradually reduces, so that a cradle would be progressively further from the façade as it was lowered.

One obvious solution, cleaning by abseilers, was immediately ruled out: it is prohibited as a cleaning strategy on health and safety grounds. So the Foster team was challenged to devise a safe and practical means of keeping the 'Gherkin' squeaky clean. The solution adopted was to install a 'garage' on level 36, just below the top of the tower. This contains a pair of motorized, two-person cradles that are run out on two rail tracks, with a section of the façade swinging back to allow them to be attached to the parallel tracks, which run around the exterior of the building. The cradle, supported on a telescopic arm, can then be lowered to clean the tower from level 36 downwards, with the problem of the diminishing girth of the building addressed by means of sockets set in the façade into which the operatives can insert restraint pins and cables to anchor the cradle and keep it close to the glazing. The lower two floors can easily be cleaned from the ground-level plaza.

The issue of how the 'top of the building' should be cleaned presented an additional challenge, since the cradles could not move upwards. The solution was a variant of the typical 'cherry picker', a five-stage extending arm with a cradle for two operatives at its end, which can traverse the dome via the external rails and extend up to 30 metres, reaching even the lens at the top of the tower.

On 28 November 2002 the official topping out ceremony was marked by a spectacular lighting display that was visible across London. Part of the display remained lit until the New Year.

Topping out came on 28 November 2002. Inconveniently, it coincided with Thanksgiving Day. Sara Fox had organized a dinner at her home in Islington, north London, and had to rush down to the site, leaving a friend to keep an eye on the roasting turkey – supplied by Skanska as a gesture of conciliation – then hurry back to receive her guests. The blue-and-green lighting installed to mark topping out was left on until the New Year. The lighting display over the holiday period not only promoted the Skanska brand, but equally left nobody in doubt that construction of the 'Gherkin' was well and truly under way.

Overleaf
Speirs and Major's lighting strategy, intended to dramatize the architecture of the building, included mood settings for the lobby and reception that vary by day and by night.

FIT-OUT

The fit-out of the lobby had always been seen as part of the commission to Foster and Partners, though there was a great deal of discussion about the treatment of the two-storey-high wall surfaces. In the end, a profiled aluminium extrusion was selected. At an early stage, Swiss Re insisted on seeing a layout of the lobby plan in the Foster and Partners car park in Battersea. As a result, the exterior walls of the lobby were moved to enlarge the space and improve circulation. The fit-out of the Swiss Re accommodation and the top of the building began in spring of the following year, six months before practical completion of the shell and core. It might have been assumed that Foster and Partners would be appointed for this phase of works, but in the event the commission for the office floors had gone in summer 2001 to bennett interior design, selected from a shortlist of three firms, with Richard Beastall as partner in charge. The choice was inevitably a disappointment for Foster and Partners, though the practice was retained to design the top-floor spaces. Sara Fox admits that she was looking for an approach rather different to that seen in some of the Foster office projects that she visited, but the decision was taken collectively by the project steering committee. One issue that had to be addressed by the fit-out design was that of the balconies overlooking the atria: in total they accounted for 4% of all the space in the building and could hardly be left empty. Foster and Partners proposed that they should be largely used as 'break out' social spaces.

The main lobby, designed by Foster and Partners, includes finishes such as the anodized aluminium wall cladding, stainless steel column covers, enamelled low-level security screen incorporating the reception desk, flamed granite, and a double-height glass façade with four revolving doors.

The main lobby finishes are carried through to the lift area, where elements such as the lift indicator are carefully detailed within the profiled aluminium wall cladding.

Overleaf
Swiss Re's office includes a boardroom on the 11th floor that seats thirty-four people. It incorporates a video-conference facility, permitting meetings to take place with Swiss Re's many offices around the world.

The fit-out design had to address the legacy of Swiss Re's previous dispersed accommodation. "Some of the people had very swanky offices and considered themselves rather superior", says Fox. "Other offices were the pits. Now everyone would have the same working environment." Beastall recalls that Swiss Re's commitment to quality was never in doubt: "Visiting their offices in Zurich, we were impressed by the quality and the elegant, minimal modernist ethos. We wanted to reflect that in our work." Swiss Re had to decide how much of the building it would occupy and which floors. It decided to settle in the lower half of the tower, since it was felt that the upper levels would be more attractive to potential tenants. The lower floors, on average the largest, also suited its business needs much better than the higher and smaller floors.

The brief given to bennett interior design included finding productive uses for the balconies on the edge of the atria, illustrated below by the client conference area on the 11th floor.

Beastall's team interviewed all the departments that were to occupy the building, assessing their requirements in terms of space and location. Open-plan office space was to be the norm, with a limited number of cellular offices. These had to be located opposite the balcony edges, which were reserved for communal facilities – coffee points, copiers and filing library areas, for instance – that would make them centres of activity and interaction, with the bonus of striking views out of the building. On level 11 the edges of the atria become informal adjuncts to the meeting rooms that occupy much of this floor. Swiss Re has invested heavily in audio-visual and video-conferencing facilities, the aim being quite simply to reduce the number of flights that staff need to make for meetings. Costs are reduced, but, equally important, the company is helping to cut out unnecessary travel, a consideration given that aircraft are such a conspicuous generator of carbon emissions. In the same spirit, all suppliers to the St Mary Axe project have been asked to provide evidence of their commitment to sustainable design.

A further issue to be resolved in the fit-out strategy was the treatment of the central core, containing lifts, stairs and WCs. "We decided to smooth it off", says Beastall. The core is clad in faceted panels to minimize the visual impact of the numerous access and riser doors that punctuate it, and is circled by a raised 'halo' of plasterboard incorporating lighting. The aim throughout the fit-out was to "celebrate the simplicity" of the building, says Beastall. Where partitions are

Swiss Re's space includes two internal staircases, one connecting the main reception on the 11th floor (below) to the auditorium on the 10th floor (opposite).

Clockwise from opposite
Eva Rothschild, *Mass Mind*, 2003, black perspex; Jorge Pardo, *Untitled*, 2003, ink-jet print on foil; Mary Heilmann, *The 9th Wave*, 1989, oil on canvas; Liam Gillick, *Revised Mediation Screen*, 2004, aluminium sculpture; Jorge Pardo, *Untitled*, 2002, ink-jet on foil (two pieces); Ian Hamilton Finlay, *An Arcadian Dream Garden*, 2004, twenty engravings on granite slabs.

needed, they are kept transparent so as to preserve the valuable vistas across the floors and out of the building. Office furniture is a range standard to all Swiss Re's offices: corporate continuity was valued. Colour is used only sparingly because "people provide the colour", says Beastall. Additional colour, it could be suggested, is provided by the extraordinary range of artworks that are dotted about the building, which are part of a remarkably rich corporate collection and a reflection of Swiss Re's commitment to patronage of artists.

30 St Mary Axe looks good from inside, but it is even more important that it reads well from the street and from neighbouring buildings. The impact of lighting

Opposite
The 39th-floor restaurant, the interior of which was designed by Paul Kalkhoven of Foster and Partners, offers elegant dining to tenants and their guests.

was potentially enormous. Again, in the floors that it was to occupy, Swiss Re specified that energy-saving should be a priority, facilitated by a control system that turns off lights when an area is unoccupied. The brief to lighting designers Speirs and Major Associates, however, was to give this aspect of the building an element of magic, reflecting the landmark status of 30 St Mary Axe. The lighting of the lobby and reception area was a special challenge, as appropriate moods for day and night-time had to be created. Equal care was needed with the restaurant and hospitality space, the crown of the building. For the office areas special circular fluorescent lighting fixtures were commissioned. The use of these fixtures is obligatory in the parts of the building let to tenants: as Sara Fox says, the prospect of lighting varying in intensity and hue from floor to floor, and of conventional strip lights "marching across the floors by night, highlighting the ceiling grids", had to be avoided. "Just look at Cesar Pelli's tower at Canary Wharf!" she comments. "A bit of a dog's dinner."

The 'top of the building' spaces, the restaurant and bar on the 39th and 40th floors and the private dining-rooms on the 38th, form the spectacular climax to the tower. They are contained within a dome, 30.5 metres in diameter, 22.5 metres high, constructed of steel and resting on the main structure of the tower. Norman Foster had successfully argued that these should be spaces for people, not mechanical services. Today it seems hard to imagine their being anything else. From the 39th-floor restaurant you look out at the most spectacular view obtainable from any London building, with the sky above you. Close by are the lifeless upper floors of the City high-rises of an earlier generation, mere containers for machinery. It was never imagined, presumably, that one day their arid flat terminations would be routinely viewed from above. Apart from tenants of the building and their guests, this is a view that has been enjoyed, by day and night, by thousands of members of the public during London Open House in 2004 and by a staggering 25,000 people who have attended social events at the top of the building in the first year since its opening.

The decision to award Foster and Partners the fit-out commission for the top of the building, along with the 34th-floor lift lobby (the point of interchange for access to the top floors and an incident on the journey from the base of the tower to the summit), provided some compensation for the Foster team's natural disappointment at seeing the majority of the fit-out awarded to another practice. But it is at the top of the tower that the Foster vision of 30 St Mary Axe is most fully realized.

The design issues affecting the 'top of the building' fit-out were extremely complex. Given the proposed use of the upper floors as restaurant and bar spaces, considerable areas would need to be allocated for cooking and preparing food, along with service risers, lifts and escape stairs and full disabled access, all within the smallest floorplates in the tower. The design of services was absolutely fundamental to the fit-out project: heating, ventilation and fire protection had to

Opposite
7 November 2003: The circular staircase linking the 39th floor restaurant and bar area under construction.

Right
The staircase completed.

be seamlessly incorporated within a determinedly minimal aesthetic. As Sara Fox says, "Norman Foster grasped the point immediately that the real issue was about external space and the views out; the interior had to be as simple, clean and empty as possible." The theme that dominates the entire 30 St Mary Axe project – the integration of structure, services and aesthetics – is very much to the fore on the upper levels of the building.

The main kitchen area is located on the 37th floor, where available space is constrained by the fact that most of the floor perimeter is occupied by the tops of the large cooling towers located at level 35, with other chunks of space accommodating plant. On floor 38 a finishing kitchen serves five private dining-rooms; more than half the floor space is occupied by escape stairs, firemen's and goods lifts, service risers and WCs. There is a spectacular (and, for some, intimidating) walk along the edge of the building to access the last of these. The angled walls of the dining-rooms reflect the need to adapt their geometry to that of the containing diagrid.

Level 39, accommodating the restaurant, is, apart from anything else, a masterpiece of space management. The total floor area is 510 square metres, of which the central core accounts for 156 square metres, and more than half of what remains is required for services and staff areas. The actual dining area is little more than 150 square metres, but it is, of course, the lofty proportions of the space that give it real drama. However, it had to be a comfortable, as well as a dramatic, interior. Air conditioning was mandatory on the upper levels of the building, where the façade is a (double glazed) single layer, but there was still the issue of controlling uncomfortable solar glare (a particular problem in the winter months) in a fully glazed space. The glass is tinted to the same degree as that in the atria lower down the tower. At one stage, it was proposed to fit a moveable internal sun shield that would follow the path of the sun, but this costly and potentially intrusive piece of machinery was dispensed with and an ingenious set of sliding shades installed on the 39th floor. They can be disposed easily to baffle direct sunlight.

The restaurant and 40th-floor bar have, of course, no ceiling, just the curved dome topped by its glass lens. Where could lighting and extractors for stale air be

Lift access to the space at the top of the building terminates at the 39th floor, so a hydraulically operated, glass-enclosed platform rises up the centre of the circular stair to allow full access to the 40th floor. The top of the stair and platform can be seen to the right in the picture opposite.

located? The remarkably modest installation surrounding the lens contains lighting and extractors; the architects' idea of what Sara Fox describes as a "disco ball" suspended in the centre of the space was not taken up. Cooled air enters the 39th floor at the perimeter and centrally behind slatted screens that mask the service areas. Further perimeter cooling is provided around the elevated bar space. This is accessed via an elegant curving stair, but it was also necessary to provide disabled lift access. The idea of a glass box, housing the lift, intruding within the bar, was judged unacceptable. Instead, a simple circular platform, within a glass enclosure was installed, similar to that used by I.M. Pei at the Louvre in Paris, which transfers a wheelchair user effortlessly to the very top of the building. The machinery is concealed behind the kitchen on the 38th floor.

The palette of materials used in the fit-out of the dining-rooms, restaurant and bar reinforces the air of restrained luxury (equally reflected in the care given to the choice of everything from table linen to cutlery). The granite used for the floors is Nero Absoluto and is also used in the WCs. A flame-retardant polyester material called Trevira, similar to that used for making trainers, is used to cover internal screens, and is impervious to staining.

30 St Mary Axe is capped by one of the most impressive modern spaces in Britain. In Foster's work, it bears comparison with the British Museum Great Court and the spectacular dome of the Reichstag in Berlin, equally vibrant celebrations of structure and natural light.

A splash of colour is provided by the back wall of the passenger lift lobbies in Swiss Re's space in the building.

Swiss Re's use of the balcony edges in its office space includes tea points and copy areas, as well as communal areas where staff can gather.

The first Swiss Re staff moved into the building just before Christmas 2003. "The trading floors, floors 12 and 14, had to be occupied during the Christmas holiday, when markets were quiet", Peter Holroyd of Swiss Re's project team recalls. "They were moving in while the lobby area was still a building site." Fox remembers the final stages of the fit-out as "horrendous – we all felt very close to the wire". Departments ready to move had to be told to delay their plans: "it was a hair-raising, nail-biting, ulcer-inducing experience. There was a huge amount of grumpiness in the organization." Fox had the full backing of the Swiss Re board to impose a new discipline on everyone moving into the tower: "They had to reduce

View from the balcony edge over a typical
Swiss Re office floor.

their storage requirement by 35% – that meant weeding out files, a tedious job." (Once the building opened, Fox kept a keen eye on the office spaces, and storage boxes left untidily against the façade were likely to be summarily removed, with a sharp note to whoever was responsible.) On the other hand, when people moved into the building, they seemed to warm to it immediately. Fox recalls: "Most people got a PC upgrade and a bigger desk, little things like that. But there was the point that the building itself was morale-boosting. People were pleased to leave it in the evening and see tourists staring up at it and taking pictures – suddenly they were working in a building that was as much a sight as St Paul's or the Tower of London."

Sara Fox remained with Swiss Re until the summer of 2005, her chief responsibility, once the building was up and running, being to co-ordinate lettings. Initially, she says, the wave of positive publicity that the building had generated was countered by rumours and simple misinformation about its specification and performance. For those who had always opposed the project, any hint that there were teething troubles was something on which to seize. "Developer in a pickle as cracks form in Gherkin", reported Mira Bar-Hillel in the *Evening Standard* in November 2003. "Cracks are beginning to appear on some of the giant glass panels wrapped around it", she claimed. In fact, some of the panels (26 out of 5000) had suffered damage in transit and had cracked on installation or, in a few cases, had been fitted with the incorrect glass by the manufacturer. As Frank Hensky of Emmer Pfenninger, the Swiss cladding consultancy advising on the cladding installation, commented: "We are talking about 40,000 square metres of glass in the building, which uses a highly customized system with a very complicated geometry. If only 20 panels are chipped or cracked, that's nothing. I've seen a lot worse on smaller projects."

There had been other misleading reports of problems with the building, some of them acquiring the status of urban myth. It was top-heavy and sinking under the weight of its upper storeys. The glass would have to be replaced with perspex. The 'spread' at the centre of the tower was far greater than planned and there was a danger that the building would split apart. All these reports were pure fantasy. In May 2005, after one of the glass panels of the opening windows fell to the ground – it emerged that a vital fixing had failed, an event reported by *Building Design* under the headline "Gherkin gasps for air after glass fall" – it was as if everyone was looking for the most progressive feature of the building to fail. (The fixing has since been redesigned and has been replaced on nearly eight hundred opening windows.) *Building Design* also reported that some tenants had erected partitions around the atria, thus making it impossible for the natural ventilation system to work. This was true – and unfortunate. But the whole point of the devolved services installation was that it allowed tenants a choice, floor by floor, and it was never the intention to impose the natural ventilation system on them. In any case, the negative comments on the building did not deter potential tenants who now include law firms, fund managers and insurance brokers.

A TOWER FOR LONDON

25 May 2004: A pyrotechnic display launched from the window-cleaning cradles marks the official opening of the building.

27 April 2004: A media open day held on the 17th floor attracted members of the international as well as British press, and included a presentation by Norman Foster.

The formal press launch of 30 St Mary Axe took place on 27 April 2004. Media coverage of the building had, of course, been intensive from the time that the designs were unveiled, and its completion was eagerly awaited. For all but a few diehard opponents the furore over the remains of the Baltic Exchange was forgotten. Far from representing a surrender to the IRA, the new tower was a bold symbol of the confidence of the City. For the City Corporation's planning supremo, Peter Rees, this is a structure that has "single-handedly changed the perception of tall buildings in London". Swiss Re, he says, "didn't set out to build an icon, but it's become a symbol of London. It's rebranded Swiss Re, the reinsurance business and the City of London – quite an achievement." Rees, it is no secret, strove hard to convince the members of the Corporation that the building would be good for the City, persuading them to lay aside doubts about its scale and form and to resolve the impasse over the ruins of the Baltic Exchange. He now feels that the project was a turning point. "We're looking at a number of really interesting high building projects in the City – Richard Rogers's 122 Leadenhall Street, for example, which looks rather like a giant cheese-grater and the

Building tall in London

30 St Mary Axe is neither London's tallest building nor even the tallest building in the City of London; at 180 metres it is a few metres shorter than the nearby Tower 42 (formerly the NatWest Tower), while One Canada Square, the central tower at Canary Wharf, is more than 50 metres taller.

Nonetheless, planning approval for 30 St Mary Axe, finally granted in the summer of 2000, proved a catalyst for other tall building projects in the City and beyond. Having supported Swiss Re's project, English Heritage opposed plans for the so-called Heron Tower (at 110 Bishopsgate), designed by Kohn Pedersen Fox, and a public inquiry was convened in 2001. The outcome was government approval for the 200-metre tower, part of a cluster of tall buildings deliberately sited in the eastern sector of the City to minimize the impact on views of St Paul's and other historic monuments. During the same year, plans for the "Shard", to be located next to London Bridge station and designed by Renzo Piano, were submitted. After a reduction in the height of the building from 390 metres to 306 metres these proposals too won planning consent after a public inquiry. Kohn Pedersen Fox's Bishopsgate Tower, submitted for planning consent in 2005, will also top 300 metres; its curvaceous form has won it the nickname of "the Mexican Wrap".

A feature of the recent wave of tall-building proposals in the City has been the involvement of world-class architects: Richard Rogers, for example, in the case of 122 Leadenhall Street ("the Cheese Grater", 225 metres high); and Nicholas Grimshaw for the 217-metres-tall Minerva Building at Aldgate. At the end of 2005 a number of other tower projects were in the pipeline for the City and its fringes, including schemes by Wilkinson Eyre, Ian Simpson and Rafael Vinoly.

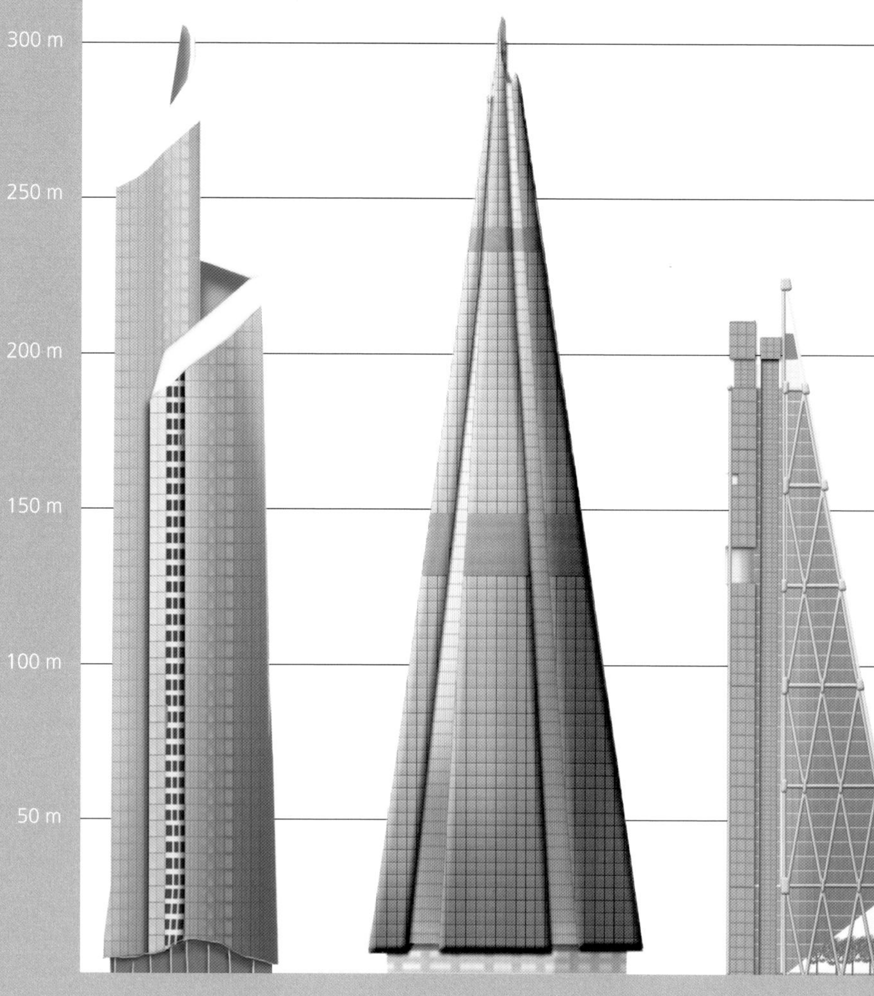

Bishopsgate Tower
Kohn Pedersen Fox
307 metres
Awaiting planning permission

London Bridge Tower
Renzo Piano
306 metres
Planning permission granted

122 Leadenhall Stree
Richard Rogers
225 metres
Planning permission granted

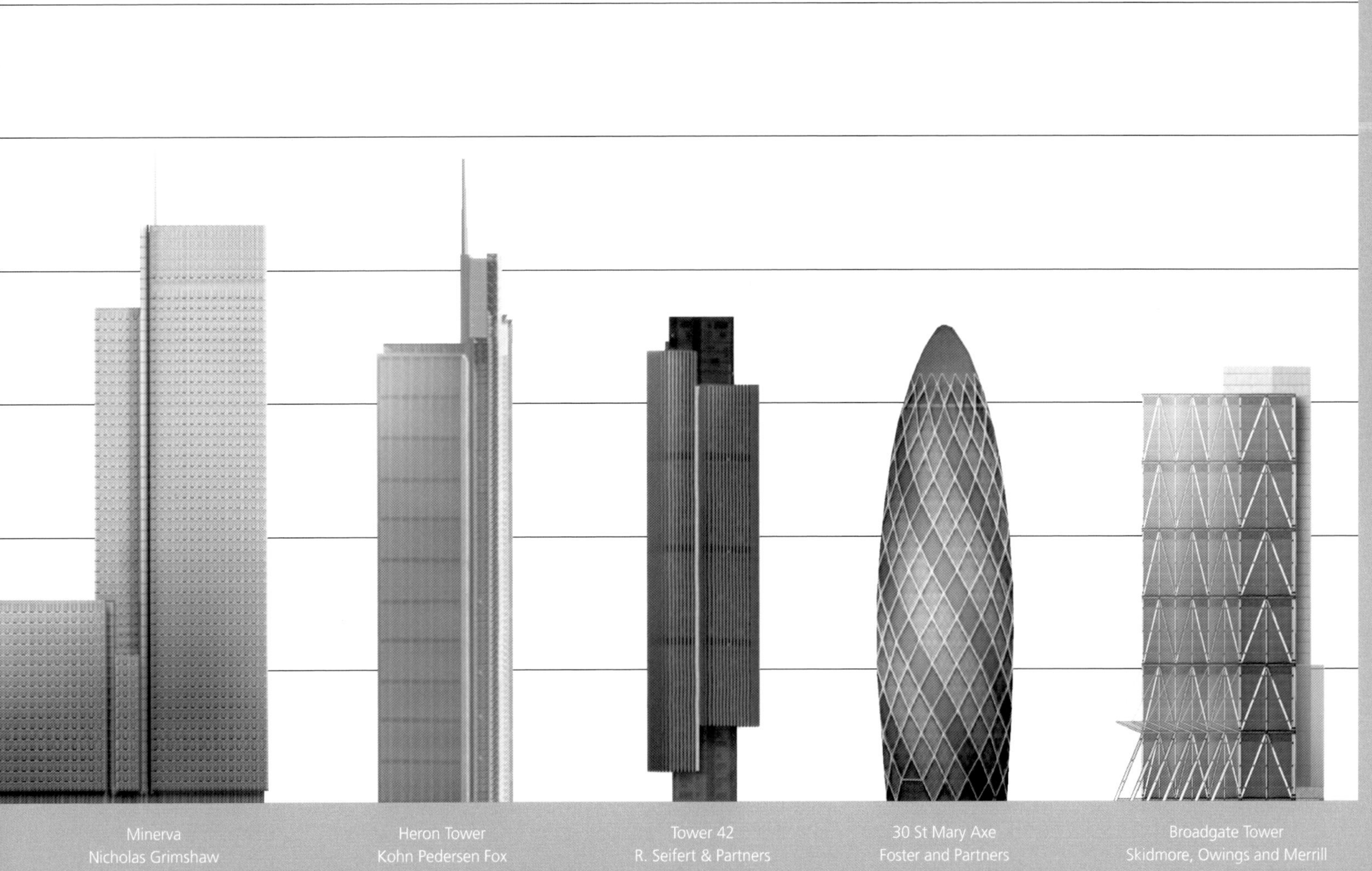

Minerva
Nicholas Grimshaw
216 metres
Planning permission granted

Heron Tower
Kohn Pedersen Fox
183 metres
Planning permission granted

Tower 42
R. Seifert & Partners
183 metres
Built 1980

30 St Mary Axe
Foster and Partners
180 metres
Built 2004

Broadgate Tower
Skidmore, Owings and Merrill
164 metres
Planning permission granted

In late 2001 an exhibition of Foster and Partners' work at Denmark's Louisiana Museum of Modern Art included extensive coverage of the design process for 30 St Mary Axe.

Overleaf
In 2004, the Royal Academy of Arts Summer Exhibition included a gallery of tall buildings curated by Norman Foster.

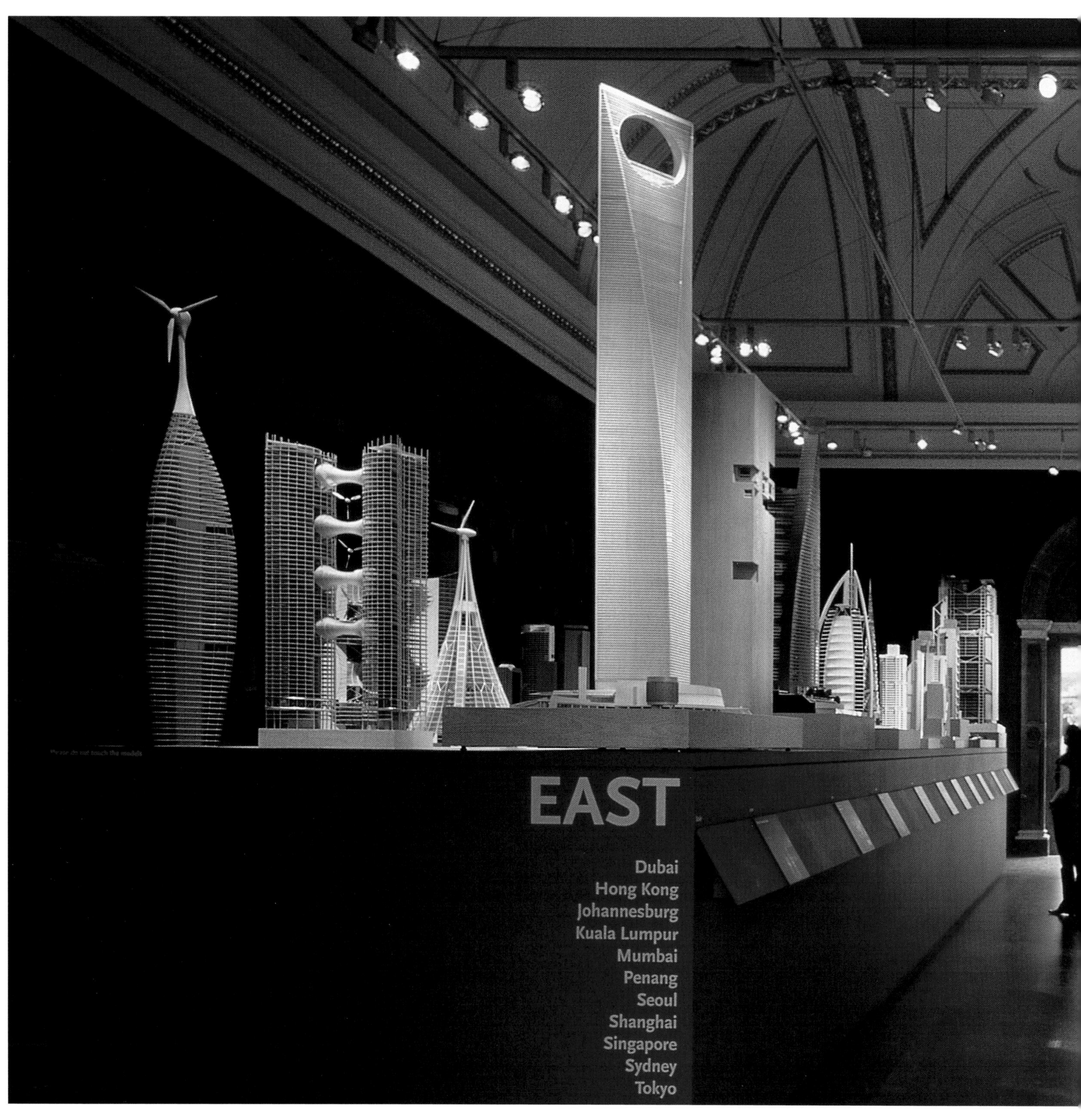
EAST
Dubai
Hong Kong
Johannesburg
Kuala Lumpur
Mumbai
Penang
Seoul
Shanghai
Singapore
Sydney
Tokyo

WEST
Barcelona
Chicago
Frankfurt
London
Munich
New York
Rotterdam
Vienna

Kohn Pedersen Fox scheme for Bishopsgate, which I compare to a Mexican wrap." A decade ago, Rees admits, most of these schemes would have had a hard ride from the Corporation: now it is receptive to proposals that have real quality and visual interest. It is the overwhelming public approval for the 'Gherkin' that has been instrumental in this change of heart. Even before it was completed, the building was being used as a symbol of the dynamism of British design, shown, in an exhibition, *Great Expectations*, at New York City's Grand Central Station in 2001.

In September 2003 Deyan Sudjic of *The Observer*, a long-standing supporter of the 30 St Mary Axe project, described the building as "the tower that ignited London's current preoccupation with the skyscraper". Compared to the Hongkong and Shanghai Bank, "a handmade Bugatti", the Swiss Re tower was "like a suave, polished BMW". Sudjic praised the "civilized dialogue" that the building conducts with its neighbours and the "intimate" plaza around it. In a memorable simile, he wrote of the tower "erupting" over the City "like a colossus, a King Kong, which, thanks to the diamond-shaped windows, looks as if it is wearing giant argyle socks". Paul May of *The Guardian*, in a piece titled 'Why I love the Gherkin', felt that the building "has the English whimsy that Lord Foster always manages to dress up as environmental awareness or high-tech visioneering". Specialist journals were as supportive as the general press. 30 St Mary Axe was, wrote Jeremy Melvin in the *RIBA Journal,* "the tall building as a work of art ... a marker for more tall buildings. It sets not just a standard but an agenda for the future, when we might all be living and working in sky cities, breathing fresh air and swooshing up and down like angels on Jacob's Ladder."

Ian Ritchie, a distinguished architect who had worked in the Foster office, sounded a more sceptical note in *Architecture Today*. The supposedly radical environmental strategy of the building would have to be tested in practice, he wrote, while the claims of the project to social radicalism were specious when there was no public access to the top floors except for those hiring the space. Ritchie confessed that he did not find the shape of the building pleasing: "one might question whether the form of 30 St Mary Axe derives from a rigorous approach to urban planning or from a desire for difference for its own sake." Peter Davey of the *Architectural Review,* ever an idiosyncratic voice, argued that the form of the building was "not an urban shape".

Ritchie and Davey were, however, rare voices of dissent in what was an overwhelmingly positive critical response that extended far beyond Britain. "The building is radical – technically, architecturally, socially and spatially", insisted the Italian design journal *Domus,* "unlike any other office building so far conceived." Its shape was "its most distinctive quality, transforming the cluster of boxy towers around it". Writing in the *Wall Street Journal*, David Littlejohn said that "the wise men and women of Zurich have blessed this narrow old lane in London's historic financial center with a sparkling, sensuous, profoundly sensible tower. Foster and

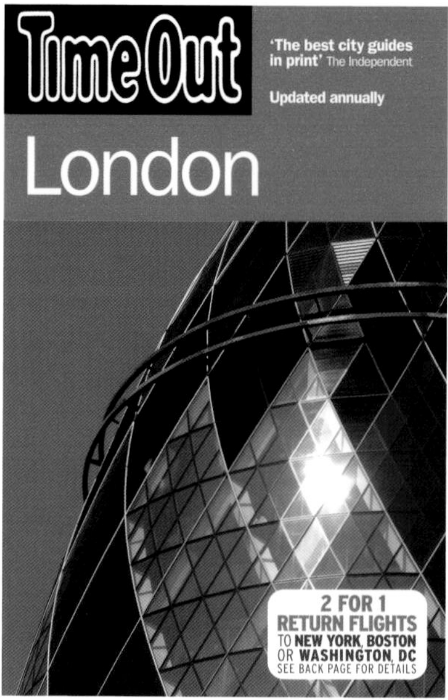

30 St Mary Axe has become so emblematic of London that it appears on the cover of Time Out's 2005 guide to London.

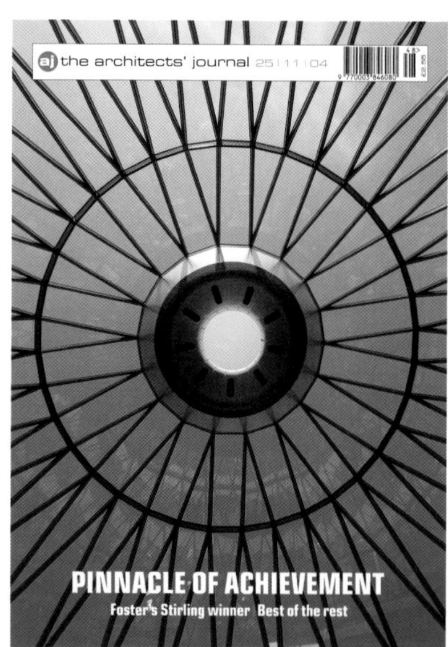

Even before the Stirling Prize was awarded in October 2004, public opinion had already shifted in favour of the building: *The Architects' Journal*, 25 November 2004 (above); *The Observer*, 17 October 2004; *The Wall Street Journal*, 13 July 2004; London's *Evening Standard*, 22 July 1999; *The Guardian*, 18 October 2004.

The Observer 17 October 2004

Gherkin is everyone's cup of tea

The tower has won over Londoners – and now the judges of architecture's top prize

by Vanessa Thorpe
Arts and Media Correspondent

IT HAS already raised eyebrows, gained its fair share of plaudits and earned an affectionate nickname from Londoners. Now the Gherkin can hold its head up high.

The annual Stirling Prize, architecture's most presti… gious award, has gone to Fos… ter and Partner's unconven… tionally shaped tower block, formally known as the Swi… …at 30 St Mary A… …building w…

list, the Business Academy at …

LEISURE & ARTS TUESDAY, JULY 13, 2004

It's a Pickle, It's a Pineapple—It's a Brilliant New Skyscraper

By David Littlejohn

London

At just 590 feet and 40 stories, the new skyscraper officially known as 30 St. Mary Axe is less than half the height of the world's 10 tallest buildings, and not even the tallest build… …But it draws instant atten… …the Thames be…

…ter and Partners' achievement sets an almost impossibly high standard for the many neighboring London skyscrapers now emerging on computer monitors.

* * *

Remember when the American soprano Deborah Voigt set off a media storm earlier this year, complaining that she had been dumped from the title role in Strauss's "Ariadne auf Naxos" at the Royal Opera at Covent Garden? She was … Voigt said, that she was too fat … "little black cocktail dress" …lected for his updated …

…that the …

12 | Architecture

A fine pickle

As Norman Foster's Stirling prize-winne… some of the most exciting sculpture of … produced by architects, writes **Jonath…**

It's not really a gherkin. It's a pine cone, or perhaps a poplar. Anyway, Norman Foster and Partners' Swiss Re building is, as well as defiantly modern, resonantly classical. All that nonsense with Prince Charles and neo-Georgian conservatism, which has been getting away with opposing the classical to the modern, distracts from the formal beauty of the skyscraper that, rightly, won the RIBA Stirling prize on Saturday night.

I don't know what the Prince thinks of 30 St Mary Axe, as it prefers to be known. Perhaps he sees in it the ominous shape of a vertical zeppelin, menacing St Paul's. It has everything that used to be scorned by the British public: radical shape, industrial materials, imposing itself on a City skyline that some argue should be reserved for Wren and Hawksmoor. Laughed at when it was announced, instantly popular when (quickly) built, this is the first great skyscraper to be built in London.

It instantly …

…nge the skyline forever

THURSDAY 22 JULY 1999 3

'If this is a gherkin, it's a very tasty one'

by ROWAN MOORE
Architecture Correspondent

THE march of … Foster …

New City Architecture
People, Places & Buildings

The building's outline now appears in a variety of images referring to London, including (top to bottom) the logo for the *New City Architecture* exhibition designed by Wordsearch/Manha in 2003; the Financial Times Companies and Markets column artwork; the logo that appears on Transport for London's journey planner website; and an Orange promotional poster for London in May 2005.

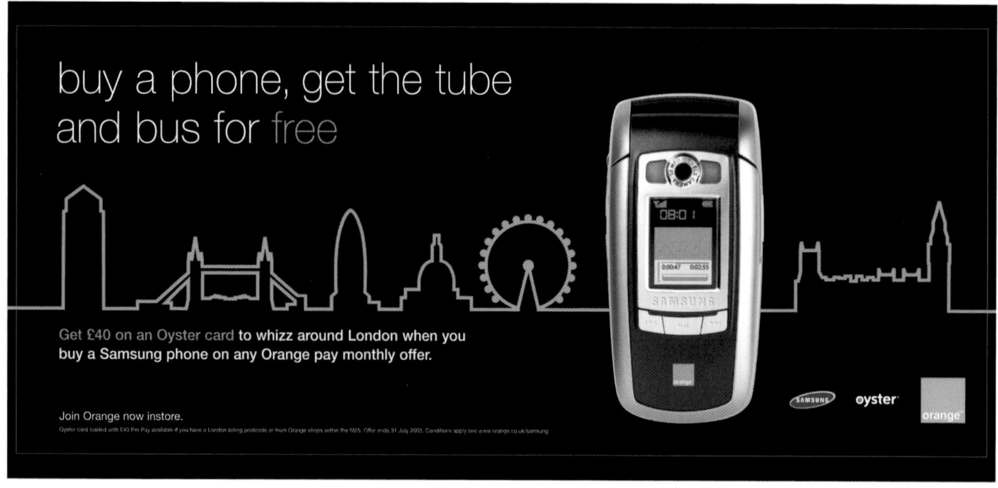

buy a phone, get the tube
and bus for free
Get £40 on an Oyster card to whizz around London when you
buy a Samsung phone on any Orange pay monthly offer.
Join Orange now instore.
SAMSUNG
oyster
orange

The Lord Mayor's Show in November 2003 included a float featuring the building that was manned by members of the team (above; photograph Georgie Gibbs), and in September 2004 thousands queued for hours during the London Open House event (above right).

In April 2005 the US edition of *Condé Nast Traveler* identified 30 St Mary Axe as one of the seven next wonders of the world. (Photographer Håkan Ludwigson)

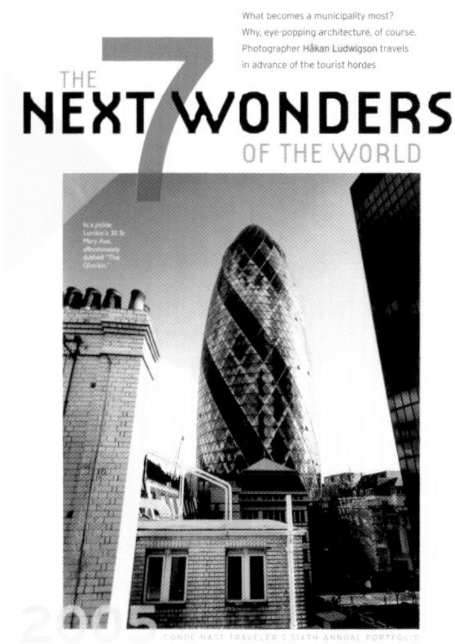

What becomes a municipality most? Why, eye-popping architecture, of course. Photographer Håkan Ludwigson travels in advance of the tourist hordes

THE 7 NEXT WONDERS OF THE WORLD

2005

CONDÉ NAST TRAVELER'S SIXTH ANNUAL PORTFOLIO

Partners' achievement sets an almost impossibly high standard for the many neighbouring London skyscrapers now emerging on computer monitors." This was, Littlejohn argued, a beautiful building that was all the more satisfying because its key features were more "the result of tough, ingenious engineering and environmental solutions than the whims of clever, tasteful artists". In April 2005 the American edition of *Condé Nast Traveler* awarded 30 St Mary Axe the ultimate accolade: inclusion in a list of "the seven next wonders of the world", alongside, *inter alia*, Rem Koolhaas's Seattle Public Library and Chicago's Millennium Park.

Londoners certainly took 30 St Mary Axe to their hearts. When parts of the building were open to the public during London's Open House weekend in September 2004, around 8000 people managed to gain admission. The queue for entry snaked around neighbouring streets, and more than 3000 people had to be turned away at the end of the day. The star attraction was the top of the building space, with its stunning views over the capital: "people would get up there and it was a real problem to get them to come down again", Sara Fox recalls. In October 2004 the building gained another accolade in the form of the Royal Institute of British Architects' (RIBA) Stirling Prize: it was "the building of the year". For the first time in the history of the prize, named in honour of the late architect Sir James Stirling, the judges, who included dancer Deborah Bull and sculptor Anthony Gormley as well as a number of distinguished architects, quickly came to a unanimous decision. They selected 30 St Mary Axe over shortlisted landmark projects such as the Kunsthaus in Graz, Austria, and Daniel Libeskind's Imperial War Museum North in Manchester.

The 'Gherkin' had qualities that enthused a lay audience as well as enthralling architects and engineers. The pulling power of the 'Gherkin' was increasingly omnipresent. The building appeared on mastheads, on posters for the London

The building was used as part of London's winning bid for the 2012 Olympics (© London 2012 Ltd), and subsequently mimicked in a Skanska trade journal advertisement.

Underground and on publicity material for London's bid for the 2012 Olympic Games (alongside the Tower of London and another new landmark, the London Eye by Julia Barfield and David Marks, which opened at the end of 1999). Early in 2005 the thirteenth edition of that tourist bible, the *Time Out London Guide,* was published, with a view of 30 St Mary Axe on its cover. The building also proved an irresistible draw for film-makers – *Bridget Jones: The Edge of Reason* (2004) and Woody Allen's *Match Point*, among others, featured scenes shot there, and the tower was soon featuring as regularly as Big Ben in other movies set in London. A documentary film, *Building the Gherkin*, directed by Mirjam von Arx, provided a vivid account of the design and construction process.

A documentary directed by Mirjam von Arx and completed in 2005 narrated the story of the building's planning and construction.

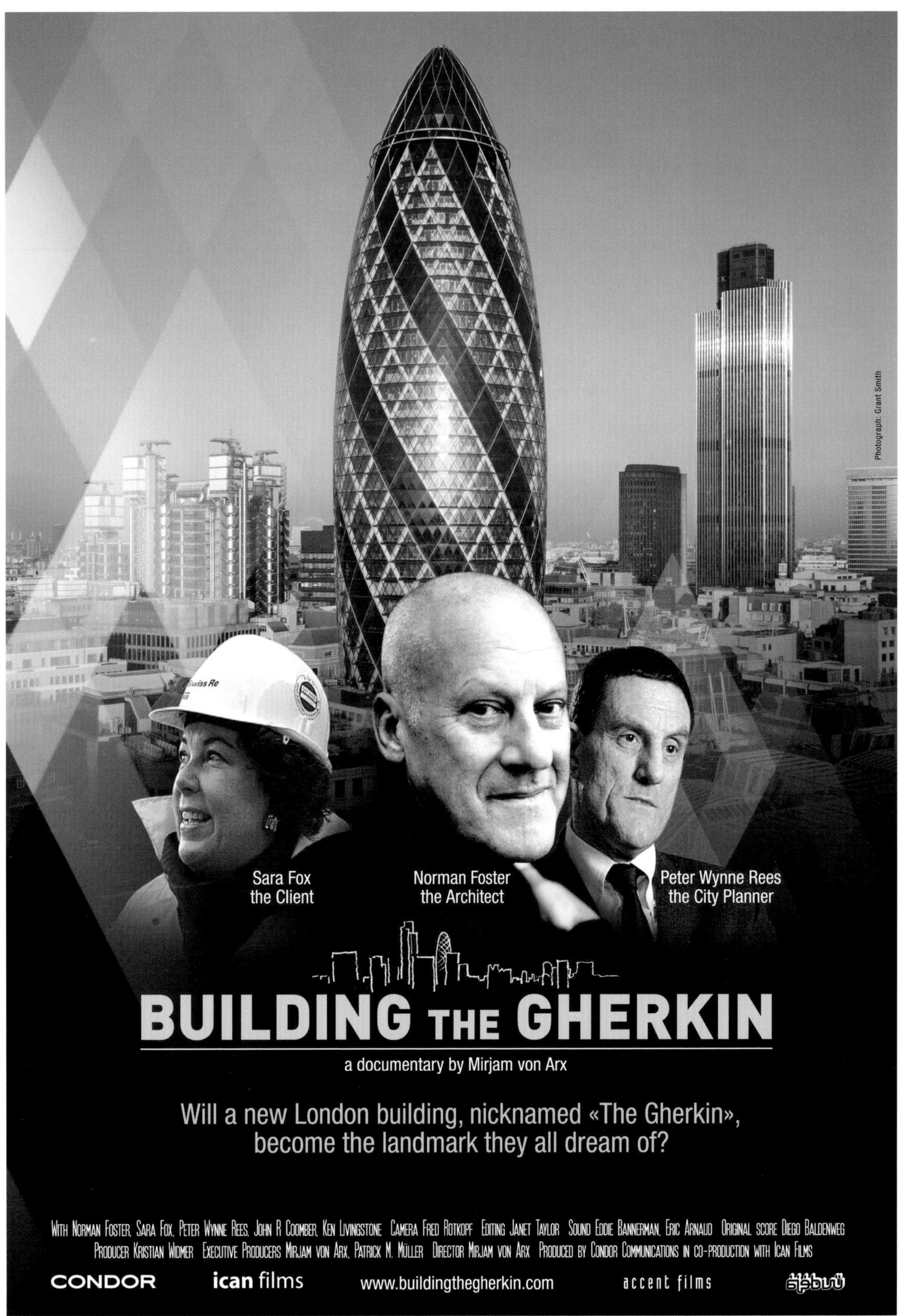

Photograph: Grant Smith
Sara Fox
the Client
Norman Foster
the Architect
Peter Wynne Rees
the City Planner
BUILDING THE GHERKIN
a documentary by Mirjam von Arx
Will a new London building, nicknamed «The Gherkin», become the landmark they all dream of?
With Norman Foster, Sara Fox, Peter Wynne Rees, John R Coomber, Ken Livingstone Camera Fred Rotkopf Editing Janet Taylor Sound Eddie Bannerman, Eric Arnaud Original score Diego Baldenweg
Producer Kristian Widmer Executive Producers Mirjam von Arx, Patrick M. Müller Director Mirjam von Arx Produced by Condor Communications in co-production with Ican Films
CONDOR
ican films
www.buildingthegherkin.com
accent films

"A perfected, stretched blob conceived as a city landmark. It started off life as an egg shape and then, after wind and structural studies, re-emerged as other natural metaphors – not only the far-fetched gherkin of the tabloids, but a more plausible and welcoming pine cone and pineapple." This was Charles Jencks's description of 30 St Mary Axe in his essay on 'The new paradigm in architecture' published in the *Architectural Review* in February 2003. Jencks, who had established a reputation as a sure-fire spotter (and promoter) of new architectural fashions with his books on Postmodernism and Deconstruction, argued that architecture was learning from "the new sciences of complexity – fractals, nonlinear dynamics, the new cosmology, self-organising systems" and abandoning the mechanistic thinking that had dominated it since the triumph of the Modern Movement. The new thinking,

The building became a setting for a number of films, including Woody Allen's *Match Point*, featuring Jonathan Rhys Meyers (below, seen with Woody Allen and Remi Adefarasin) and *Basic Instinct II: Risk Addiction* featuring Sharon Stone (opposite, bottom) and David Morrissey (opposite, top), seen on set within the building.

The building as a coffeepot, by Chris Madden.

essentially pluralistic, was reflected in the work of Frank Gehry, Daniel Libeskind, Peter Eisenman and others, and in that of the 'blobmeisters', among whom Jencks ranked Foster, on the strength of the Swiss Re project and the Sage Music Centre (2004) at Gateshead, north-east England. "Mainstream architects … produce suggestive and unusual shapes as a matter of course, as if architecture had become a branch of surrealist sculpture." The pretence of functionalism was being abandoned and architects were setting out to create icons.

Compared variously to a spaceship, zeppelin and torpedo as well as to a green pickle, 30 St Mary Axe had obvious iconic quality. In his book *The Iconic Building* (2005) Jencks returned to this aspect of Foster's tower, describing it as a "cosmic skyscraper". In an interview with Norman Foster, published in the book, Jencks pursued the issue of symbolism, with Foster insisting on the essentially practical

In February 2003 Andrew Riley painted a watercolour entitled *The Gherkin*, which became a postcard printed by Boomerang for free distribution in London's coffee shops and wine bars (above). The Charities Advisory Trust offered their version of the 'Gherkin' for sale as part of their 2004 Christmas card collection: *The Gherkin* by David Higham for Card Aid © Card Aid.

rationale of the project, which reflected, he said, "very considered responses to the perceived needs of the building in the space of the City of London … on that particular site". The conversation seemed, in the end, inconclusive.

Gehry's Guggenheim Museum in Bilbao, Jørn Utzon's Opera House in Sydney and Enric Miralles's Scottish Parliament building in Edinburgh could all be described as iconic buildings: each carries with it a great weight of symbolism about national identity and renewal. Will Alsop's Peckham Library, another Stirling Prize winner, was visually extraordinary, yet its exuberance was part of its mission in boosting the morale of a rundown area of south London. But why should an office building have such ambitions?

Foster's rational exposition of the project carries increased weight in the context of its environmental and low-energy agenda and of the increasing use during

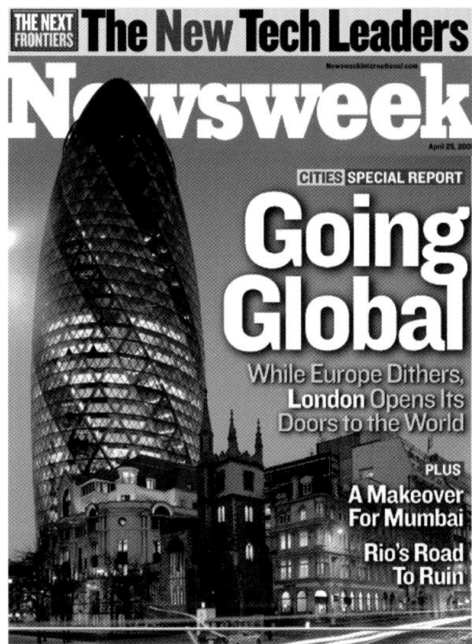

Left to right
The 25 April 2005 issue of *Newsweek* featured the building on its cover to illustrate a story on London's financial markets (photographer Jason Oddy). A July 2004 advertisement by the sporting-goods supplier, Cotswold Outdoor, cleverly wrapped the Gherkin in a sleeping bag. On a more serious note, the French publication *Archicréé* featured the building on its cover in the May/June 2004 issue.

the 1990s of computer modelling as a design tool. Such Foster projects as the Reichstag dome, the British Museum Great Court and, less successfully, the London City Hall point the way towards what Chris Abel has called a "new vernacular". For Abel, as for Jencks, 30 St Mary Axe is a radical, if not a revolutionary, building, a symbol of the transformation from machine age to information age. Foster saw the use of the computer to develop the form of the tower (though it was more a product of physical modelling) as marking not only "a quantitative change to the design process in terms of efficiency – it represents a qualitative change: the speed with which alterations can be made to a design generates a far greater degree of creative freedom". The lessons of 30 St Mary Axe fed into subsequent high-rise projects including the Manhattan Hearst Tower (2002–05) and the unbuilt 'kissing towers' proposal for the World Trade Center site. Far from being a reiteration of the ideas of the Commerzbank and ARAG towers, the Swiss Re tower's radical geometry pointed the way towards a new vision of the sustainable high-rise.

30 St Mary Axe is one of a dozen or more major City of London office projects completed by Foster and Partners since the mid-1990s. Several of them – Moorhouse and No. 1 London Wall, which 'book-end' London Wall, for instance – are conspicuous for their pursuit of a dynamic visual imagery that seems to lack the practical rationale of 30 St Mary Axe. Indeed, the finest of these City office projects is arguably that in Gresham Street, close to the Guildhall. The Miesian discipline of this building is admirable, confirming Peter Rees's judgement that "this is architects' architecture". Internally, the stepped floors recall the diagram of Willis Faber, though the project makes no claims to being particularly environmentally progressive. All these other City projects are essentially developer-led. As Foster has remarked again and again, great buildings need great clients. And with Swiss Re, he found one.

BUILDING CREDITS

CLIENT, OWNER/OCCUPIER: Swiss Re

ARCHITECT: Foster and Partners

Norman Foster

Stefan Behling
Grant Brooker
Michael Gentz
Rob Harrison
Paul Kalkhoven
Robin Partington
Paul Scott
Ken Shuttleworth
Hugh Whitehead

Francis Aish
Tim O'Rourke
Gamma Basra
Jason Parker
Geoff Bee
Ben Puddy
Aike Behrens
Simon Reed
Ian Bogle
Narinder Sagoo
Thomas Brune
Sebastian Schoell
Julian Cross
Michael Sehmsdorf
Joel Davenport
John Small
Ben Dobbin
Robbie Turner
Chris Kallan
Neil Vandersteen
Jürgen Küppers
John Walden
Paul Leadbeatter
Tim Walpole-Walsh
Stuart Milne
Richard Wotton
Jacob Nørlov
Helen Yabsley

CONSULTANTS

Project management: RWG Associates

Cost consultant: Gardiner & Theobald

Planning consultant: Montagu Evans

Legal adviser: Linklaters

Urban design and conservation consultant: The Richard Coleman Consultancy

Structural engineer: Arup

Mechanical and electrical engineer: Hilson Moran Partnership Ltd

Environmental engineer: BDSP Partnership

Fire engineer: Arup Fire

Lift engineer: Van Deusen & Associates

Cladding consultant: Emmer Pfenninger

Façade access: Reef UK

Lighting: Speirs and Major Associates

Acoustics and AV consultant: Sandy Brown Associates

Catering consultant: Tricon

Traffic engineer: Arup Transportation

Landscape architect: Derek Lovejoy Partnership

Urban movement consultant: Space Syntax Laboratory

Information technology: PTS

Security: VIDEF

Planning supervisor: Osprey Mott MacDonald

Swiss Re office design: bennett interior design

Interior construction management: Kontor GTCM

MAIN CONTRACTOR

Skanska Construction UK Ltd

SUB-CONTRACTORS AND SUPPLIERS

Piling: Cementation Foundations Skanska Ltd

Demolition: Keltbray Ltd

Monitoring and surveys: Skanska Technology Ltd

Substructure and superstructure: P.C. Harrington Contractors Ltd

Steel frame: Victor Buyck-Hollandia Joint Venture Ltd

Metal decking: Richard Lees Steel Decking

Fire protection: Dragonchain Ltd

Mechanical, electrical and plumbing: Skanska Rashleigh Weatherfoil Ltd

Curtain walling: Schmidlin (UK) Ltd

Top of building curtain walling: Waagner-Biro Ltd

Extract fan cowling: Waagner-Biro Ltd

Specialist furniture (lobby): Marzorati Ronchetti

Bespoke fabric wall system: Art Andersen A/S

Solar shading: Art Andersen A/S

Bespoke platform lift: Metalbau Luckerath

Dry lining: Lightweight Plastering & Drylining Ltd and BDL Drylining Ltd

WC fit-out: Swift Horsman Ltd

Passenger lifts: Kone plc

Architectural metalwork: Glazzard Ltd

Specialist furniture (top of building): Permasteelisa

Cleaning access equipment: Street CraneXpress Ltd

Specialist engineering (top of building): Marzorati Ronchetti

Structured cabling: Dimension Data

Blockwork: Bansal Building (London) Ltd

Stone paving: Stirling Stone (Management) Ltd and Stonewest (top of building)

Pre-cast concrete: Mallings Products Ltd

Temporary electrics: Woodlands Site Electrical Services Ltd

Tower cranes: Select Plant Hire Company Ltd

Hoists: Universal Builders Supply Ltd

Logistics: Clipfine Limited

Scaffolding: Anglewest Ltd andBow Scaffolding (Southern) Ltd

Temporary gantry steelwork: Rees Engineering Services Ltd

Bespoke GRG ceiling: James and Son

Ceiling: James and Son

Suspended ceilings: Barrett Ceilings Ltd and Clark & Fenn Ltd

Joinery (top of building): Howard Brothers Joinery

Specialist joinery (Swiss Re offices): Benchmark

Raised floors: Kingspan Access Floors Ltd

Bespoke catering equipment: Berkeley Projects

Insulation: British Gypsum-Isover

Ironmongery: Allgood

Door closers: Dorma

Door seals: Lorient Polyproducts

Entrance doors: Boon Edam

Acoustic wall panels: Decoustics

PICTURE CREDITS

The illustrations in this book have been reproduced courtesy of the following copyright holders:

Archicréé p. 212 (right); *The Architects' Journal* p. 202; Mirjam von Arx p. 207; The Baltic Exchange pp. 15, 19, 51 (top and bottom); Birds Portchmouth Russum Architects pp. 5, 74; The Bridgeman Art Library p. 12 (bottom); David Bromley (published in *Financial Times*) p. 204 (second from top); Markus Bühler p. 36 (left); Charities Advisory Trust p. 211 (right); *Condé Nast Traveler* p. 205 (bottom); Peter Cook/VIEW p. 18 (top right); Clive Coote p. 208; Cotswold Outdoor p. 212 (centre); Paul Davis (published in *The New York Times*) p. 213 (left); Richard Davies p. 26 (right); DDA Public Relations Ltd/Blow Up p. 209; Carolyn Djanogly p. 37 (left); *The Evening Standard* p. 203; Norman Foster pp. 9, 61, 66, 67; Foster and Partners pp. 9, 13, 23, 26 (left), 27, 42, 46, 47, 61, 68–69, 70, 75, 78 (top), 83, 84 (bottom), 95, 98, 106–7, 113 (top), 154, 155, 164, 193; Chris Gascoigne/VIEW p. 43 (right); Dennis Gilbert/VIEW pp. 21, 22; GMW Partnership/Corporation of London, Department of Planning and Transportation p. 20 (bottom); Goddard & Gibbs/Phillida Shaw p. 51 (centre); Guardian Newspapers Limited pp. 10 (photographer Dan Chung), 203; Guildhall Library, Corporation of London pp. 12 (top), 17; Louis Hellman pp. 53, 213 (right); John Hewitt p. 99 (top); Hilson Moran pp. 80, 99 (bottom); Hufton & Crow pp. 6–7, 105, 172, 174, 175, 176–77, 178, 179, 180, 188, 189, 190–91, 222–23; Hulton-Deutsch Collection/CORBIS p. 16; London 2012 Ltd p. 206 (left); Ian Lambot p. 12 (top right and bottom); Louisiana Museum of Modern Art p. 198 (top); Chris Madden p. 210; Rudi Meisel p. 24; National Maritime Museum pp. 48, 50; New City Architecture p. 204 (top); James Newman (skyscrapernews.com) pp. 196–97; *Newsweek* p. 212 (left); *The Observer* p. 203; Open House, Architecture Education Charity p. 205 (top right); Orange p. 204 (bottom); Andrew Riley p. 211 (left); SAVE Britain's Heritage p. 43 (left); Sectorlight Sutton Young p. 83 (bottom); Skanska UK p. 206; St Ethelburga's Centre for Reconciliation and Peace p. 20 (top); Grant Smith/VIEW pp. 2–3, 56–57, 81, 84 (top), 85, 90, 91 (bottom), 92, 93, 100, 104, 108–109, 110, 111, 112–13 (bottom row), 114, 115, 116, 117, 119, 120, 121, 122–23, 124, 125, 126, 127, 128, 129, 130, 131, 132–33, 134 (top and centre), 135, 136, 137, 138–39, 140, 141, 142–43, 144, 145, 146–47, 148–49, 150, 151, 152–53, 156, 157, 158–59, 162–63, 166, 167, 168, 169, 170–71, 173, 184, 194, 214–15; Henk Snoek/RIBA Library Photographs Collection p. 18 (top left); Space Syntax Laboratory p. 76; *The Sun* p. 18 (bottom right); Swiss Re pp. 30, 31, 32, 33, 34, 35, 36, 40, 181, 195, 205 (top left); *The Times*/The Baltic Exchange p. 44; Time Out Guides p. 202 (top); Transport for London p. 204 (third from top); *The Wall Street Journal* p. 203; Nigel Young/Foster and Partners pp. 12 (top left), 25, 28, 29, 35, 37, 38–39, 52, 54, 59, 62, 63, 64, 65, 73, 77, 78 (centre and bottom), 79, 82, 86–87, 88, 89, 91 (top), 94, 96–97, 102–103, 118–19, 134 (bottom), 160, 161, 165, 182, 185, 186, 187, 198 (bottom), 199, 200–201.

The publisher has made every effort to trace and contact copyright holders of the illustrations reproduced in this book; they will be happy to correct in subsequent editions any errors or omissions that are brought to their attention.

INDEX

Page numbers in *italic* refer to the illustrations